PRAISE F

THEY CAN KILL YOU BUT THEY CAN'T EAT YOU

"... AN INSPIRATIONAL BOOK FOR CAREER WOMEN."

—New York *Daily News*

Dawn Steel made history as the first woman to run a major motion picture studio. The hit movies she worked on throughout her career include *Flashdance, Awakenings, Top Gun, The Untouchables, The Accused, Flatliners, Ghostbusters II, Fatal Attraction, Cool Runnings, Sister Act II,* and the restored *Lawrence of Arabia.* She absorbed strategies from the powerful; her network of friends and business relationships includes Streisand, Stallone, Cruise, Cher, Madonna, Costner, Foster, and Scorsese. But behind the glamour is a story of astonishing setbacks and hard-won truths: Dawn discovered that "they can kill you but they can't eat you" after she lost her job while giving birth to her daughter. Now Dawn Steel shares the priceless experience of making it—as a woman—in one of the most ruthless businesses in the world.

"Hypnotically frank.... Steel tells her story straight out ... peppering it with just enough kiss-and-tell.... this book is about power—who gives it, who takes it away.... A winner for sure...."

—*Kirkus Reviews*

"Anecdotes and advice from a high-concept career...."

—*The New York Times*

"One of Hollywood's most resilient filmmakers premieres her own version of her rise and fall and rise. . . . The life of Dawn Steel unspools like a movie."

—*New York* Magazine

"Her lessons on how to be twice as tough, twice as innovative, and twice as nervy to succeed as a woman in a man's world are applicable to any business where men call the shots."

—Don Ienner
President, Columbia Records

"Dawn Steel survived Hollywood with a vengeance. . . . Steel won't litter Hollywood Boulevard with corpses. . . . But at least she's making the sharks nervous."

—*Mirabella*

DAWN STEEL
ON GETTING THINGS DONE
If they throw you out the front door, you go in the back door. And if they throw you out the back door, you go in the window. And if they throw you out the window, you go in the basement. And you don't ever take it personally.

ON DEALING WITH IMPOSSIBLE PEOPLE
Never try to teach a pig to sing. You waste your time and you annoy the pig.

ON DEAL-MAKING

If you are negotiating from a place of desperation, you're dead. You have to be willing to let it go.

ON FEAR

Deal with it. Get in its face.

ON POWER

When I was younger, men were my role models . . . and it was men from whom I thought I'd derive my power. But I have to say that in the history of the world no man who was sane or sober ever gave his power away to a woman.

Dawn Steel

They Can Kill You But They Can't Eat You

Lessons From the Front

POCKET BOOKS

New York   London   Toronto   Sydney   Tokyo   Singapore

POCKET BOOKS, a division of Simon & Schuster Inc.
1230 Avenue of the Americas, New York, NY 10020

ISBN: 0-671-73833-X

First Pocket Books paperback printing August 1994

10 9 8 7 6 5 4 3 2 1

*For my mother, Lillian,
and my daughter, Rebecca*

To laugh often and much; to win the respect of intelligent people and the affection of children; to earn the appreciation of honest critics and endure the betrayal of false friends; to appreciate beauty, to find the best in others; to leave the world a bit better; whether by a healthy child, a garden patch or a redeemed social condition; to know even one life has breathed easier because you lived. This is to have succeeded.

—Source Unknown

Contents

Contents

BOOK THREE

Tempered Steel

Foreword

> What has been forbidden to women is anger, together with the open admission of the desire for power and control over one's life . . . because this has been declared unwomanly. . . . Women must turn to one another for stories. They must share the stories of their lives and their hopes and the unacceptable fantasies. . . . To put it simply, we must begin to tell the truth . . . to one another.
>
> —Carolyn Heilbrun,
> *Writing a Woman's Life*

My story is far from a Hollywood fantasy. It might sound like one, though, if you don't look deeper: a girl from a struggling, lower-middle-class family grows up, gets through high school, drops out of college when she runs out of money, has no idea what she's going to do with her life, gets a job as a receptionist, and winds up running a major motion picture studio. Sounds exciting, doesn't it? Even glamorous, right? Well, the truth is, there is some glamour and excitement in this story; and a lot of lessons. On my journey up the corporate ladder, I learned plenty.

This is a story about anger (mine), pain (mine) and power (theirs). It's about being called tough, ballsy, aggressive, unfeminine and shrill by people who have never met me and by some who have. It's about closing my office door to cry when I'd seen one more mean article calling me Attila the Hun. Or worse, it's about hard choices like abortion and having a baby. It's about learning to keep your friends close and your enemies closer . . . about navigating the treacherous waters of the corporate world. It's about finding your strength.

When I was younger, men were my role models. From my father and my brother to the brilliant and powerful men who were my mentors in Hollywood, it was always men I turned to. And it was men from whom I thought I'd derive my power. But I have to say that in the history of the world no man who was sane or sober ever gave his power away to a woman.

Today, thank God, there are female role models. And the admission of the desire for power and control over one's life is no longer forbidden.

Only recently, I've been able to see that my obstacles, once I understood them, became signposts on what was to be my path. Ironically, I feel that everything that might have sabotaged me has helped me, instead.

I hope the lessons in my story will help accelerate the trip up the ladder and reduce some of the anxiety, offer some insight and create a spirit of optimism and hope. For women trying to get off the receptionist's desk . . . for women who want to be valued for cherishing their roles as mothers . . . for corporate vice presidents who are as sick as I was of wanting to be one of the boys . . . for women who are wondering, as they're conquering the next step, So what do I do now?

This is a story of a woman who climbed the male ladder of success. A woman who learned that you cannot expect anyone to rescue or take care of you. This is about learning that the most important resource you have is you. And that you can find success, power and happiness . . . as a woman. That much I know. I still have a lot to learn, but I finally feel as if some lessons now belong to me so profoundly that I can share them with others. Women must begin to tell the truth of their lives to one another.

This story is my truth.

—Los Angeles, June 1993

They Can
Kill You But They
Can't Eat You

Introduction

I CAN REMEMBER EXACTLY WHERE I WAS WHEN I FIRST learned about my demise.

I had just closed the door to the middle stall of the second-floor ladies' room in the Administration Building at Paramount (the Admin Building, as it is known to its denizens), when two sets of footsteps entered, taking positions on either side of me. I heard a zipper unzip and then voices; I recognized them as belonging to two secretaries from the production department:

"She's dead," said the first voice.

"Who?" asked the other.

"Dawn."

"She's dead?!"

"Cold and almost in the ground," said the first voice too definitively.

"You're kidding?"

"Nope. Tanen hates her. She's never going to make it . . ."

Hearing your obituary is stunning; hearing it when you're stuck in a bathroom stall is, at best, humbling. I was reduced to silence, frozen with dread. There it was: I was dead.

And what made it worse was that what I was hearing was an echo from some critical, tireless voice in my own mind—a voice that always said, "You're never going to make it!"

In a decade and a half, I'd gone from working as a receptionist in the garment industry to being president of production at Paramount Pictures. I had just started to learn what power was—how to get it, how to wield it, what it costs, what its rewards are—when a new administration was brought in to Paramount. I was desperately trying to make the transition from the Barry Diller–Michael Eisner passionate team-playing management techniques to the mercurial, unpredictable, but nonconfrontational ambiance of the Frank Mancuso–Ned Tanen reign. This new corporate palace was filled with intrigue, murky plots and backstabbing, and there was no question that a lot of it was directed against me.

I had this habit: whenever I was in doubt, in big doubt, which was often, I'd throw the *I Ching,* the Chinese book of prophecy. I'd ask it a question, like, "When am I going to like my job?"

No matter what answer the *I Ching* provided, it always included the word "perseverance." As in: "Quiet perseverance brings good fortune."

Which meant absolutely nothing to me.

The night of the ladies' room incident, I threw the *I Ching,* hoping for a word of advice, a verdict, a "pay no attention to what you hear in ladies' rooms" sign. In its usual cryptic fashion, the *I Ching* at first answered: "The Receptive." What the hell did that mean? But when I read the explanatory text, I saw the phrase "Furthering through perseverance."

It was hard not to take the hint. This perseverance thing was coming up all too often, like constantly, in my life. But what did perseverance mean in this context? Pursuit? Not giving up?

It's only recently that I've come to understand that perseverance is a quality possessed by a lot of successful people. *It is not only an obligation to yourself, to pursue, to not give up, but it is also a form of vitality.* That's what this book is about: Perseverance.

In those days, the Frank Mancuso–Ned Tanen Paramount days, I lived in a constant state of anxiety that I would fail, that I might not be able to respond adequately to the new politics and demands at the studio. And living in that state made me hate my job.

I tried to snap out of it, telling myself that I was in forward motion. I had more than a hundred people reporting to me, I was working twelve-hour days, seven days a week, and I had just gotten pregnant with my first child, an event I had prayed for for years.

I tried to tell myself I was absolutely where I was supposed to be: I was forty years old and I was about to have it all.

I tried to ignore the echo. Maybe I was just paranoid. Why wouldn't I make it? I had had tremendous success with both *Flashdance* and *Footloose*. I had, in production, *The Untouchables, The Accused, Beverly Hills Cop II, Star Trek IV, Fatal Attraction* and *Top Gun*. And I was developing, among others, *Ghost* and *Good Morning, Vietnam*. I was doing well.

Even my new husband, Chuck Roven, a film producer and usually my best adviser and strategist, was not diabolical enough to correctly decipher the writing on the wall. "Maybe you're hormonal," he'd say to me when I would tell him about my troubles at work. He was right. I was.

But as I got more and more pregnant, the politics at Paramount became more and more vicious and harder to write off to hormones or paranoia. I became determined to show the men who were the new top management that I could survive the toughest working climate. I was determined to be so motivated, so effective, and so totally competent that they would have to come around.

Months after I overheard my obituary in the bathroom, I was in the hospital giving birth to my little girl. The following morning I read in the trades that Tanen had brought in someone who would not be reporting to me, but who would report directly to him. I wasn't quite fired but it was your quintessential Hollywood humiliation and setup: I had the choice of staying on, keeping my title and my salary but having less authority, or leaving.

This was not a new maneuver in Hollywood; it's a kind of coup that often follows a studio-palace intrigue, and it's always planned and executed without the person's knowledge. But as far as I knew, this was the first time it had ever happened to a woman in labor. Then again, I was the first woman to have had a baby while she was head of production.

But in the palace scheme of things, that's irrelevant. *Woman or man, if you want to play in this ring, you have to be able to take the punches,* wherever they're given, whether in the boardroom or the labor room. The only trick, as it turns out, is to survive.

When I first got the job as president of production

at Paramount, my friend Ron Meyer (now president of the powerful talent agency C.A.A.) gave me some advice. He said, *"Keep your friends close and your enemies closer."* It was a perfect Ronnie-ism. I laughed and promptly forgot it.

But boy, was he right. And the moment I learned the consequences of forgetting that lesson was that day in the middle stall of that second-floor ladies' room.

But to paraphrase Mark Twain, "The reports of my death had been greatly exaggerated."

Actually, it took another six months for them to kill me. . . .

BOOK ONE

THE DAWN
OF
DAWN

1

HAPPY?
WHO SAID ANYTHING
ABOUT HAPPY?

1946. HARRY TRUMAN IS THE PRESIDENT. JOE LEWIS IS THE
champ. Ethel Merman belts out hits in *Annie Get Your
Gun*. Radio musicians protest television, fearful that
the new technology will replace radio broadcasting.
The big movies are *The Big Sleep, Great Expectations*
and *It's a Wonderful Life*. The big pop music hit is
"Zip-a-Dee-Do-Dah."

A name like mine has to be reckoned with. My
whole life, people would say, "Dawn Steel, what a
name!" My father was a weight lifter, the "Man of
Steel," and that's where my last name came from: he
changed it from Spielberg. He also gave me my first
name. Apparently, just before I was born he was up all
night, and as he watched daylight break, the name
Dawn Steel hit him.

The other great gift I got from my parents was my hair. "I mean, you had a full head of hair when you were born," said my mother. "It was growing on your head, your neck, your shoulders, and they told me, 'Don't worry, it will come out in the first bath.' I bathed you three times a day." So, at birth, I looked like Chewbacca in *Star Wars*. But it turned into a tremendous asset. (No, I don't have hair on my back anymore.)

As a kid, even in my worst moments of teenage insecurity, I always knew I had great hair. It was the first thing I liked about myself. For a long time it was the only thing I liked about myself. Yet people who didn't know me but who knew my name always figured there must be a pretty tough cookie under that mane of hair. Appearing to be someone I wasn't has been both a psychological calamity and a great advantage—a calamity because I never got the protection and reassurance that everybody needs, but a great advantage because it forced me to ignore my fragility and fight harder in the world.

I've been called a lot of names. The first time I met Robin Williams, he said: "Don't Steal? What kind of a name is Don't Steal?" But better Don't Steal than some of the other names I've been called. The Queen of Mean. Tough as Steel. Steely Dawn. The Creep of the Crop. Steel Balls.

I was born in the Bronx. It was not a storybook event, believe me. As she came out of the anesthetic, my mother did not think life—or her new baby— looked so wonderful. She was terrified to see her doctor looking as if he had just come from a butcher shop, a clue that I had been delivered by a C-section that would leave her with a horrific scar the full length of her abdomen. In those days they carved you open from sternum to pubic bone. She used to show me the scar and say, "Look what you did to me. I almost died." It was said as a joke. But that's not how I heard it. I used to look at her terrifying abdomen, truly believing mine would someday look like hers.

But, aside from my name and my hair, and my stomach notwithstanding, I got other great gifts from my parents. From my mother, I got the notion that women are equal to men, a novel idea in the 1950s. From my father, I picked up a sense of humor and learned not to be afraid of men. Some of the other things my parents gave me I am still recovering from. Like being five-foot-three and a half. And having zero self-esteem.

I used to think it was their fault. It wasn't. And what I learned is to stop blaming my parents. Stop blaming anyone. But that took a long time.

I didn't begin to know this until I was in my early thirties and heading for Hollywood. And it wasn't until I began to write this book that I came to understand why my parents did what they did. It used to be too painful to look back any more than was necessary. But sooner or later you have to dig into your past and face it. I looked and there were some jewels in the garbage. And some fantastic lessons. I finally have compassion for my parents and, in many ways, I see them as heroic. I know, too, that my story is, in many ways, their story.

I was born into a family that didn't have a lot of legends. Legends were a luxury they couldn't afford.

Both sides came from Russia. My mother's parents, Rebecca and Nathan Tarlo, were from the Ukraine. My father's parents, Rebecca and Louis Spielberg, came from somewhere between Kiev and Odessa, or so my father thinks. My grandmother, when she married Nathan Tarlo, was told by his Aunt Fanny that she was marrying into a family that had loaned money to the czar. She was marrying a somebody.

The revolution was a great leveler. Whose side were they on? Their own, say my parents. The czar or the revolution, the Jews got killed either way. They had to get out. They say that my father's parents came over on a boat, steerage, and stood up, literally, the whole way from Russia. And that his mother was forced to leave behind a sick daughter, who died or was murdered by the Cossacks. As a result, his mother died young of a broken heart.

The story about my mother's mother is that when Grandma Tarlo's mother died, she was separated from her two sisters, given silver candlesticks as her inheritance and put on a boat for New York. "What is mind-boggling is how they got from Russia to the boat. They had to cross all of Europe," said my mother. "They were children."

For legends, that's about it.

My mother's people changed their name from Brebtarlov to Tarlo at Ellis Island and moved to the Lower East Side of New York, where my mother was born. Then they moved to the Bronx. My mother told me that her mother was the most insecure person in the whole world. Her sister and her mother-in-law were always putting her down for hooking my grandfather, having babies right away and ruining the future of a mathematical genius.

These Jews from the Old Country, all they did was work! "Keep your head down and work" was their byword. They were all socialists. "Not communists," says my mother. "If you weren't rich, you were a socialist, because that was the workers' party." My grandfather Tarlo was a peddler who did anything he could to earn a living. To get her children out of the Bronx in the summer, Grandma Tarlo worked for room and board as kitchen help and as a maid at a hotel in the Catskills.

My grandparents' circumstances created a tradition of social insecurity in my family. Their almost insurmountable problem was that they didn't speak the language. My grandfather was said to be a highly talented mathematician but there was no way for him to communicate. They had some very hard times. These Russian Jews who came over during the revolution did not understand the concept of happy. When I complained to my grandmother one day, "I'm not happy," she said, "Happy? Who said anything about happy?"

My grandmother stopped being a maid when they'd saved enough money to buy a job. How do you buy a job? They purchased a little newsstand on Wall Street. My grandmother made tuna, chicken and egg sandwiches, and sold them from the stand from six in the morning until dark. Those sandwiches were so successful the couple was able to sell the newsstand at a profit and move to Miami Beach. There, they opened a little luncheonette counter. More chicken sandwiches. They learned English, sort of.

In my memory, my grandparents were always very old and very short. They didn't die, they just got so short they disappeared.

When they lived in Coney Island we visited them often. I'll never forget my grandmother's 3-D floral slipcovers on the couch. It was almost like tapestry, the flowers popped up. But the couch was also covered with the thickest plastic you ever saw in your life. I always figured she thought I was going to urinate on it.

"You're so funny looking," my grandmother would exclaim in her Russian-accented English whenever she saw me. But I knew she didn't mean it. My grandfather was so quiet, but whenever my brother and I walked into the room he melted. My grandparents were colorful and warm and accepting. This was unconditional love before there was a theory about it.

On my father's side, things were different. My father's father was an angry and mean man named Louis Spielberg with whom we didn't have much connection. My father had been more or less estranged from him for a long time. He had much more money than my maternal grandparents, and lived in a much nicer apartment, but there was never any place for us in his home.

My father grew up in the streets of Williamsburg, Brooklyn's slum. He was out on his own at a very young age because his mother, Rebecca, died when he was five. Have another baby, they had told her, it will cure the depression over the daughter you left behind. So she had my father, but it didn't cure the depression, and he knew it. "She died of a broken heart," my father told me many times. In those days, everything was blamed on a broken heart. My father vaguely recalls her trying desperately to get well, pushing herself to get out of bed and wash floors.

It broke my heart when my father told me, just

14

recently, that the only person who loved him as a child was Sadie, the housekeeper who looked after him until his father remarried. That explains so much.

Grandpa Louis Spielberg was in the retail fabric business, jobbing textiles. Buy for $1, sell for $1.20. Sell first, buy later. I think this is where I got my negative feelings about selling as a line of work, as if it would forever be associated for me with my grandfather's disagreeable and ruthless temperament. My grandfather was left with two sons, my father and his older brother, Sam, and neither one of them ever got a drop of love from him.

Grandpa Spielberg was sadistic in some ways, at least in my mind. Or let's just say that his history doesn't speak all that well of his abilities in the interpersonal department. The same matchmaker found him five wives. Four of them died. So my father had five stepmothers. The one my father knew best as a child was Bessie Taylor—or Mrs. Taylor, as my father always called his stepmother. She cared much less for my father than she did for her own children. But at least he had a home. His brother, Sam, ten years older, was kicked out by Mrs. Taylor and developed emotional problems. As my grandfather went from one marriage to another, he had no room for Sam. And after many years of abuse, getting kicked out of his home was Sam's final blow. His fragile psyche could not withstand it. He cracked. My father's most tragic memory was the night he was called to the police station and had to commit his brother to a mental institution. My father was only seventeen years old.

"It killed me to have him committed," my father

told me, "but I wanted to save his life. He wouldn't have survived on his own." Uncle Sam is still alive, and he's now in his nineties.

"It's a miracle," I keep saying to my father.

"That's what keeps me sane," says my dad.

To compensate for the emotional deprivation he became something of a playboy, and went out with a lot of models. He became a weight lifter. In the high school magazine he was written up as the Man of Steel for prying open the locked bars of the school gates with his bare hands to let the kids in on weekends. I always had the feeling that by diverting his energy into this area he was able to withstand the lack of love at home.

And did he have dreams! He dreamed of becoming a concert baritone. But he had no encouragement, or money, for lessons. He also dreamed of becoming a great athlete—a football or baseball player, a professional wrestler, and there he had a bit of a head start: the school coach came over to his house and pleaded with my grandfather to keep him in school because of his athletic potential. There were scholarships.

But my father blew that dream on a football field in Brooklyn. He was trying out for a semiprofessional football team when he got bashed and bent like a pretzel by some big guy. He tore the ligament in his left knee while he was flying through the air. His football career was over. He quit school at sixteen and got a job delivering teeth for a dentist.

"I never met anyone who delivered teeth," said my mother. "It was one of the things that attracted me to your father," she teased. That, and his muscles. He was a hunk. When he was seventeen, he moved to the 92nd Street Y, which had an in-house gym. He

16

worked and worked at bodybuilding, and became—
Mr. New York City! My father, Mr. New York City.
My father, Mr. Manhattan. My father, the Man of
Steel. Eat your heart out, Arnold Schwarzenegger.

Nat Steel and Lillian Tarlo met at a dance at the
92nd Street Y. My mother was working in an office.
Where else? My father was going back into jobbing
textiles, like his father, but working out was his real
passion. At a bodybuilding contest, my mother overheard somebody say, "If he flexes his back muscles
another inch, they'll have to expand this gym."

They dated for four and a half years. They danced a
lot. In a picture I used to stare at when I was a kid,
they are dancing the tango and he is lifting her up in
the air. Her toes are pointed. They look gorgeous.

Their wedding sounds like something straight out of
Guys and Dolls, with rabbis, bookies and a terrible
family fight. The wedding was at home because my
mother's mother said, "If I don't see it, I won't believe
it."

My father gave up his double life a month before I
was born. In business he had been using his legal
name, Spielberg. But among his friends he played out
his dreams as Nat Steel, the professional weight lifter.
I was coming and a kid can't have two names. So they
chose Steel. As for my first name, my mother never
believed him when he talked about his revelation as
day was breaking. "I always thought Dawn sounded
like a show-girl kind of name he must have seen on a
billboard," she says. "It always sounded to me like a
stripper." But he won.

The day I was born, my mother asked my father,
"What does she look like? Because with a name like
Dawn Steel, she better be beautiful." My brother

Larry was born a year and a half later. He was beautiful.

The message I got from my mother at the time was, "You're the smart one. Your brother's the pretty one." And because he truly was, there was no reason not to believe her. My mother thought this was high praise, but it made me feel like the star in *The Ugly Duckling Meets Cinderella*.

On top of that, practically from the moment he was born, Larry possessed an effortless charm. He was completely charismatic. Everyone adored him. And so did I.

At the beginning, we lived in nice places. My father was doing well when I was born, and we lived at 411 West End Avenue, on the Upper West Side of New York City. When I was seven months old, we moved to Merrick, Long Island, to a nice, bright little house. My mother felt that living in the suburbs was the same as being sent to Siberia, but it was easier than raising children in New York City, and I was happy in the backyard.

My father was doing so well that, in 1952, we moved to Rockville Centre, to a house I recall in my child-memory as Tara in *Gone with the Wind*—one of those nouveau antebellum houses with two huge pillars on the front porch. The house was filled with antiques and sun. I always felt warmed by it. I loved that house. I had my friends on the block, Roger and Bart, and the two Kathys to play with. I was a regular kid.

I remember my father would come home from work on the train every night, throw me up in the air, and tell me he was the King of the Giants. He was the King of the Giants to me. He was the biggest of the big. He was mythic. I adored him.

The idyll ended when I was nine. In one day, everything changed. My father had a nervous breakdown.

No one told me what was wrong with him, it didn't have a name. He was in his room. But because the doctors didn't know whether he might become violent, my mother kept him away from us. And so it was as if my father just vanished, disappeared.

Once, I snuck into his room. And something happened by his bedside that I blotted out until just recently. I don't know if he actually said it or if I just felt it, but the memory is of him saying, "Go away. You can't help me." I didn't see him again for months.

All I wanted was to help my father and I couldn't. He wouldn't or couldn't let me. And it filled me with rage.

The man I adored had closed me out. I remember nothing that happened for the next two years. I climbed into a black hole that I didn't come out of for a very long time.

My father's breakdown was the most important event of my childhood. For better and for worse, it made me who I am. It scarred my femininity, which altered not only my relationships with men, but also my view of my place in the world.

"You think you're missing two years?" my mother said when I talked to her about the gaps in my childhood. "Think what happened to me during that time."

She had a point. The events that triggered my father's illness were devastating for her. My parents had spent their last dime fixing up their beautiful home. They had joined The Engineers' Country Club to play golf. They had two babies. Enough leisure time. A piece of the American pie in the postwar period of prosperity and high energy. A nice life.

Suddenly, they were wiped out. My father's best friend and partner had stolen all the corporate assets and bankrupted his business. My father had no job. No office to go to. The IRS was after him for taxes on the money that was stolen. If my father didn't have the money, how could he pay taxes on it? This was a question that didn't interest the IRS. It was like *Catch 22*—they wouldn't listen to anything logical. My mother explained they had no money. The IRS said, "Pay."

The immediate trigger for my father's breakdown came when my parents were driving past a school where boys were playing football on the field. He had been deeply depressed about the embezzlement. My mother actually saw it happen when he saw those kids playing ball. It was the last straw. The last thread that tied him to his dreams finally snapped, as his ligament had on the football field.

He entered a terrible period of rage and depression. Shock treatments and therapy calmed him, returned him to a functioning state. But my father had moved into his own zone. He closed off. He built a barrier to protect his fragile heart.

Every family tragedy is a sort of *Rashomon,* and every member of the family suffers her or his own tragedy. When we talked about it years later, my mother said: "You know what? I had no one to talk

20

to." She was right. It was a heartbreaking, lonely struggle for her. She hoped no one knew. But kids know. The neighbors knew. We knew. I wish she could have talked to us.

The atmosphere of our lives now became less like Kurosawa and more like Dickens. Or less like *Gone with the Wind* and more like *Halloween II.*

And, on Halloween, 1957, we moved from the *Gone with the Wind* house to a dark, damp little rented house in a crummy neighborhood on the wrong side of the tracks in Great Neck, Long Island. It was the creepiest place I had ever been in. There was so much shade no grass could grow, only mold and mildew. No sun came in the house.

It was here that I became a tomboy. Obviously, being a girl didn't work so I decided to become a boy. I never owned a doll. I became the pitcher on the softball team, instead. I also began to swim competitively. I wanted to be with the boys. I wanted to be a boy.

My memory clicks on again as I started sixth grade in Great Neck. The teacher made me stand in front of the class and said, "This is Dawn Steel. She's new."

I felt so vulnerable, naked and alone. In many ways, the damage was done: my father was not available to me, my mother was too busy fighting our survival battles to notice my loneliness.

I did okay in school: I got B's and C's. Not good enough, in my mother's eyes or in my own. I lost my voice. When the teacher called on me, even if I knew the answer, I often couldn't get the words out. There was nothing wrong with my vocal cords. I wasn't physiologically paralyzed, but I was psychologically crippled.

Sunday nights were filled with anxiety. I dreaded going to school because I lived in constant fear that someone would call on me. A remnant of this in my adult life was that I never went to work on Monday mornings without anxiety. It felt like the beginning of the school week.

I began to believe that I was no good at learning. I was ashamed of being inarticulate. At home, although my mother told me I was the smart one, she didn't have the time to let me finish a sentence. I felt intellectually inadequate. Even at the height of my success, I was always intimidated by people who were better educated and better spoken than I was. The seeds of my lack of self-confidence had been planted.

In the fifties, in my home, self-confidence was a luxury that was not on anybody's mind as we struggled to survive financially and emotionally in the wake of my father's collapse.

We didn't have a sense of a future. The world had shrunk to the immediate present, the next ten minutes or ten minutes ago.

My father had retreated to the narrowest range of emotion, as if the more he let himself feel, the more vulnerable he would be to losing control again.

The only time he ever cried in front of me was when his father died. When my grandfather got cancer, he came to live with us. My brother Larry gave up his room and slept in the dining room for a couple of years. Not that there was any gratitude or sympathy or much interest in return. Grandpa Spielberg just tolerated us around the house, as if we were one more nuisance to him. He was not much warmer or courteous to my parents either.

Yet when Grandpa Spielberg died, I walked into the kitchen and my father was leaning on the counter, his head in his hands, crying. I couldn't believe my father was crying over the death of this cold, nasty man. Years later, I asked him how he could feel any compassion for a man who gave him no love. What my father said to me I'll never forget. "He was my father," he said. *"When your father dies, you'll cry, too."*

Yes, I will.

Despite everything, I knew that he loved me. Even in his withdrawal and depression, I knew I was still the apple of his eye. He lit up when I walked into the room. He still does.

As fragile as our relationship was, the thing my father gave me was that I was always comfortable with men. I loved men. I still love men. I read a wonderful book recently, Maureen Murdock's *The Heroine's Journey*, and recognized myself in one of Murdock's categories, "a father's daughter"—"a woman who has identified primarily with the father, often rejecting the mother, and who has sought attention and approval from the father and masculine values." In some ways, it's a good thing to be a father's daughter. If you're not lucky enough to get this ease with men from your father, you have to learn it if you want to function in the world as it's presently constituted. Because *you cannot hold your own with men if you are dealing from fear.*

The disadvantage, of course, is that at some point you must reckon with all you are missing on the feminine side, or you will never be a whole person. But that would come much later for me.

I also had love in spades from my grandparents. In

the winter, my parents took us by train to see them in Florida. My grandparents were extraordinary together. There was enormous respect, love and empathy between them. They had been married sixty years and they still walked down the street holding hands. When my grandmother got sick, my grandfather literally swallowed her medicine, and vice versa. We all thought it was so cute, but it was also deeply touching.

They lived modestly on Social Security in a tiny one-room apartment. But the apartment was always immaculate and sunny, in contrast to my dark home. It always smelled great there because my grandmother was always cooking for us. When Larry and I walked in the door, my grandparents just beamed. For us, it was heaven.

At home, it was less fun. The family crisis weighed my mother down with bitterness and resentment. The IRS was hounding her to pay the back taxes. They told her that, since she was a healthy young woman, she should go to work. She took a job as an accounts receivable supervisor for a small electronics company in nearby Port Washington.

They say she was vivacious, charming, smart and lively. I never saw that. I can't remember my mother wanting to have fun.

Only later did I learn what a terrible time it was for her. In those days, when women got married they thought they were going to be taken care of. My mother was unprepared for being the provider. She was angry. Angry and terrified: was her husband going to come out of it or was he going to be an invalid for the rest of his life? She must have been scared to death wondering how she was going to take care of two small children and an incapacitated husband, keep a roof over our heads and pay back the IRS. I wish I had known then how brave my mother was.

With treatment, my father improved, but he was afraid to go to work. He was scared of everything. My mother made light of it and said, "Come on, you bum. Go to work." She took him to the Long Island Railroad and practically pushed him on the train. She sat in the interviews with him and he got work, buying and selling textiles. Then my mother stepped back and my father pushed himself, with all of his might, out of his black hole and back into the world. After all, he was the Man of Steel.

But he was now earning much less money, not enough to support us. And he could have worked from now till doomsday and not made a dent in the IRS debt. So it was still up to my mother.

When she went to work, she was offered less than sixty dollars a week. But seventy dollars was the bare minimum, in her mind. So she risked everything: "Okay, you don't think I'm worth it. Pay me nothing at the end of the first week. You tell me what I'm worth." They did wind up paying her the seventy dollars. And she got a raise every month after that. In eight years, my mother became general manager, the only female executive in the company, with nine department heads under her. I knew she had been a success when she told me, "They all resented me." What impresses me even now, thinking about it, is that my mother believed in herself enough to take the enormous risk to get the seventy dollars, at a time when she could ill afford to work for an entire week for no pay, and possibly lose the job.

Maybe there's a lesson there. Today, there's a lot of honesty about what's wrong with mother/daughter relationships and how badly served we are by our mothers' passivity and submission to an unfair system. But maybe we should give our mothers a break. *Maybe our mothers are better role models than we think.* Mine was.

My mother even faced down the IRS, and won. Sick of the harassing calls at seven-thirty in the morning, and of forever paying off a debt that wasn't really ours, she stormed down to the Long Island IRS office and said, "I'm not paying you anymore. Write it off as a bad debt." And they did.

Through all this, my mother maintained her dignity. At the time it looked like keeping up with the Joneses. She cared about appearances. Not just in terms of status, but also aesthetically. She dressed well. She wore suits to work. That's how I still remember her now, in those suits, coming home from work, kicking off her heels, too tired to cook or play with us.

It was very important to my parents that no one "knew." They were very private people. And proud. When we had to move from the *Gone with the Wind* house to the damp, Dickensian house, my mother moved all the furniture with us. It was a weird juxtaposition: an ugly little house filled with beautiful antiques. Every house we moved to, the antiques went with us, the emissaries of my mother's hope and dignity.

My mother was a perfectionist, which was manifested in her constant criticisms. She was desperate for us to be as good as we could be. To achieve, to excel in school, to stand up straight, to hold my stomach in and to keep my hair off my face. And then there was the tragic subject of my arms.

One day, my mother took me shopping for a prom dress at May's—the lowest of the low discount places. I tried on a lot of dresses; the one I liked best was black chiffon and sleeveless. It was $11.99 and we could afford it.

We had just about decided to take it when the saleswoman came into the dressing room. She gave me a once-over and said, "You can't wear that. You have fat arms!"

I did not buy the dress. In fact, from that moment on, I never wore a sleeveless anything, ever in my life. No one has seen my arms in years except my husband. Do you think Barry Diller would be where he is today if he was worried about fat arms?

I'm still trying to forget some of the wrongheaded "lessons" I learned, the lessons all girls of my generation learned about their bodies, lessons that are so hard to unlearn.

My six-year-old daughter, Rebecca, of course, has the most perfect body in the history of bodies. She has the most perfect everything in the history of everything. There is nothing that she does or doesn't do that I don't praise. I will make other mistakes she will hate me for, but this is not one of them.

2

I'D LIKE PAPPAGALLOS IN ALL THE COLORS, PLEASE

1960. JOHN F. KENNEDY IS ELECTED PRESIDENT OVER RICHard M. Nixon by a narrow margin. Emily Post, arbiter of etiquette, dies, as does Oscar Hammerstein, master of the musical. A hootenanny ends the Newport Folk Festival and on the last day a large audience gathers to discuss folk's new popularity. Chubby Checker sings "The Twist." Kirk Douglas gets crucified in *Spartacus*. The big movies are *Exodus, The Apartment* and *Psycho*.

For me, adolescence was characterized not only by the usual hormonal catastrophe—pimples, and I had them big time—but also by the development of relentless willpower. Trying to win my mother's approval made me a perfectionist.

Perfectionism makes you a control freak. It makes

you an exasperating pain in the ass—and I was one. But perfectionists learn how to do things right. We are obsessed with excellence. I was always trying to get it right. In areas where I couldn't—like in school—I retreated altogether. In areas where I had a chance, I was invincible. When my mother gave me a summer job in her office, I became the best calculator, switchboard and mimeograph operator in the Western world. She was a perfectionist herself, which is probably why all you could get was faint praise from her.

When I got to know Barbra Streisand, she told me about something that happened when she got her Crystal Award. The Crystal Award is a recognition of achievement given by an organization called Women in Film, and recipients have included many of the most distinguished female participants in the business. I was there the day Barbra got her Crystal Award and she made a remarkable speech about women treating other women better, which earned her a sincere standing ovation.

But afterward, Barbra told me later, she said to her mother, "So, Ma, what'd you think?"

And her mother shrugged and said, "So, what's not to like?"

Just like my mother would have said.

The only remedy is to learn to love yourself. I needed my mother's approval so much. But this is an important lesson: *You're not free in life until you're free of wanting other people's approval.*

I didn't realize it then, but you can learn to give yourself approval. If your mother can't or won't praise you, you've got to find something to love about yourself.

For me, it was my hair. The hair that had scared my

mother at birth grew thick, sort of tawny auburn, and dramatic. And, although I was painfully conscious that I was deficient in the breast department—what good were those training bras if I couldn't train any breasts to come out of my chest?—I thought I did have a nice butt. Some of the boys at school let me know that. I was actually flattered when the high school football team yelled "Charge at the crack of Dawn!" as they approached the line of scrimmage.

As I moved through high school, the sixties were unfolding as the greatest decade of protest and civil unrest in the history of America. The month I turned fifteen, the Berlin Wall went up and the first American soldier was killed in Vietnam. While I was in the eleventh grade, Puff the Magic Dragon was slyly celebrating the new drug culture, *The Feminine Mystique* was inspiring the American women's movement and Martin Luther King inspired the American civil rights movement with "I have a dream." As I graduated from high school, in 1964, Mary Poppins and the Stones symbolized the growing war of values.

Where was I? I was oblivious to what was blowing in the wind, aware of only the most momentous events, the absolute landmarks. I was shattered by President Kennedy's assassination. And as millions of my peers were being galvanized into militant protest, I was unconscious.

As I was growing up on Long Island, the playground of the upwardly mobile, money seemed to be at the root of all our trouble. It made my mother bitter, and I empathized and identified with her frustration and shame, so that I, too, was bitter and embarrassed that we couldn't afford much. My parents, in their desperation, tried to do the best for us by putting us in what they thought was the finest public school system on Long Island. Even if they couldn't afford much they moved to Great Neck, one of the more affluent suburbs. The problem it presented was that all my friends were very wealthy. The result was that for years I felt like a kid whose nose was pressed against the window, and from those years of feeling powerless and shamed I've kept a lifelong susceptibility to humiliation.

Nothing rubbed it in more than having to do the laundry at the laundromat. That started when my mother went to work. There was no washing machine in our house on Bellingham Lane. So when I got my learner's permit I loaded up the car with the laundry of the week, and I drove to the laundromat. A family of four has an awful lot of dirty laundry. It was piled up so high in the back of the car I couldn't see out the rearview mirror.

One day, on the way to the Laundromat I stopped at my neighborhood soda fountain, Fredericks, for an egg cream and ran into the guy I was madly in love with. His name was Bernie Strauss. He was a college boy—the "older man" in my life. I'd had a crush on him for a long time but he didn't even know who I was. That day, he finally talked to me. I was afraid he could hear my heart pounding. After we'd chatted a while, he said, "I'll walk you to your car." I said, "Great." Suddenly, I saw the car, and my brother's dirty underwear topping the mountain of filthy laundry in my back seat. I panicked.

I can still feel what it felt like. I can still remember

my fear that Bernie Strauss—that paragon of elegance and wealth—would witness my shame and degradation and would view me forevermore as the girl with the dirty underpants in her car.

So I did the logical and mature thing. I steered him in the direction of someone else's car. Fortunately, in those days, nobody locked their cars. So I got in, said good-bye to Bernie, waving while he walked away. I did not return to my own vehicle until he was safely out of sight.

But by then, I was so unraveled that as I backed out of the parking space, I smacked into a tree. Which I took as a sign of God's punishment for my dishonesty.

My father was better and now doing just well enough to move us to the south side of town where my parents could afford to play golf again. (Lake Success had its own free municipal golf course.) I was in the eleventh grade. I had to transfer schools again. And my mother and I hated the house. It was less moldy and dark than the one on the north side of Great Neck, but it was a small house that sat on the Long Island Expressway. The traffic noise was deafening.

I was ashamed of our house, so most of the time I went over to my friends' houses. I loved their big houses. I wanted what they had.

I wanted great clothes. I wanted to go to Florida on spring break and ski on winter breaks. I wanted to go on a teen tour of Europe. I wanted a nose job. And I wanted my best friend Leslie Matusow's dress, a chartreuse dress with jewels around the neck, sleeveless. She had great arms. I wanted her arms.

But more than anything, I wanted Pappagallos. Do you remember those shoes from the early sixties—the Pappagallo flats everybody wore? All the really hot girls in my town wore them. They had them in all the colors.

I came home from school one day and told my mother that I was desperate for some Pappagallos. My desperation must have been eloquent, because my mother actually went into her purse for money for one pair.

I said, "But Ma, I want a bunch of colors. I want all the colors that the other girls have."

"Sorry, honey. You can't have the same as they have," said my mother.

So that afternoon, I went to Pappagallo's. And instead of coming home with only a pair of shoes, I came home with a job. I got my dumb shoes and a very important lesson: *I could have all the things all the other girls had, but I would have to work for them.*

I worked every afternoon while my friends went to Squires, the neighborhood deli, for French fries and Cokes. I didn't mind. I figured out that all my friends' mothers who came into this shoe store felt sorry for me because I was selling shoes while their daughters were eating French fries. They bought a lot of shoes from me and I was on commission. . . .

Once I figured out how to get the Pappagallos, what mattered most in the eleventh grade at Great Neck South High School was getting to be a Kiltie.

You have to understand that Kilties were not the orthodox "Rah, rah, go team go" cheerleaders, not your run-of-the-mill pom-pom girls. Kilties were more sophisticated, hipper girls who, at halftime, would do a kind of Rockette-like syncopated routine.

They wore plaid kilts. And they were the coolest girls in town. They were a precursor to the Laker Girls.

As soon as I started Great Neck South High School, I yearned to be a Kiltie. I knew only one girl who was a Kiltie, my new friend Laura Janiger. And it wasn't long before successful fantasies of myself as a Kiltie or terrible, wounding fantasies of never being a Kiltie began to take up most of my psychic space.

But the only way I was going to find out if I could make it was if I tried out. And I was terrified of auditioning. So terrified that I developed a perspiration problem. Nothing worked. There was nothing on the market that kept me from ruining all of my blouses and sweaters with huge wet stains of sweat. The only alternative was the dreaded dress shields, a kind of sanitary napkin for your armpit. It was my last resort. I took it.

I spent weeks sweating and preparing for my audition, a routine choreographed to the theme song from *The Bridge on the River Kwai*. Nothing else mattered; just the bliss or heartbreak that awaited me at the end of my audition.

Finally, the day came and I sweated so badly on that gym floor, in front of all the other Kilties, I was afraid I'd slip on my own perspiration. But I didn't. And I made it. I was a wet Kiltie. But I was a Kiltie.

It was the biggest personal triumph of my life. I wasn't rubbing my nose against the window looking in anymore. I was in. In the group. In with the in-crowd.

Basketball was huge on Long Island in the 1960s. And on the day of the big game between the two rivals, Great Neck South and my old school, Great Neck North, I was almost beside myself with excitement. It was halftime and the Kilties lined up on the court to do their show. There we were, in all our glory. White turtleneck sweaters, white knee-high socks, sneakers with pom-poms and, of course, our signature, short, flippy little kilts, pleated green and black tartan kilts held together by a giant safety pin. We were happening, lined up like the Rockettes, arms linked behind each other, a flawless line of kicking Kilties rotating in a 360-degree wheel.

As I turned, I saw faces turn toward me with a look of shock. Then they started to laugh. They were laughing at me. What was happening? As the wheel rotated, I passed people who were covering their faces with their hands. Heads were shaking. Finally, I saw my brother, making desperate gestures to get my attention, pointing to my kilt.

I looked down. What kilt? Oh, my God! It was gone! The pin had come undone, my kilt had fallen off, and I'd been kicking up a storm in my black underpants. In the pre-Madonna mid-sixties, it was a big deal to let your undies show. My brother saw this. My boyfriend saw this. Everybody saw this. No one at Great Neck South would ever let me forget it. When I graduated, in the yearbook where they bequeath gifts to every student, they willed me a box of safety pins.

Despite my occasional misadventures, I was popular. I never let anyone know that I was shy. But the act worked and I was well liked. I think it's because I was funny—an antidote, perhaps, to the pervasive darkness at home.

I had been going with Ray Marcantonio. It was a relationship my parents did not approve of. In a big way. Yes, Ray Marcantonio wasn't Jewish.

He became my father's least favorite person in the hemisphere. In a big, big way.

I think my father was worried that I was too young, that I might be having sex—which I wasn't—and that I would get pregnant—which I didn't. But what he focused on was Ray not being Jewish. He set curfews. Nine o'clock. And when I broke them, I was forbidden to see Ray at all. I dated Ray secretly through most of high school.

To some extent it must have been partly to annoy my father, to get his attention. But also, Ray was very, very cute, a great dancer and a big star fullback. He called himself the Galloping Guinea. I loved the fact that he was interested in me. As I got older I wore my boyfriends like armpieces, showing them off the way men show off models, to make myself look better. Ray was my first armpiece.

But lying to my father was a big deal. The George Washington story about chopping down the cherry tree was a paramount parable in my house. My father was obsessed with the issue of lying. You could do almost anything, but if you lied to my father you were in major, major trouble. He had a strong sense of right and wrong, good and evil. We weren't religious—not in a traditional sense—but he made it clear that God had a big book in which everyone had a page. At the top of my page in this big book it said "Dawn Steel" and everything I did during the year showed up, good on the right side of the page, bad on the left. When I got caught stealing a lipstick from Woolworth's—on a dare from my friends—it showed up on this page. When I got a mediocre grade, it showed up on this page. When I argued with my father, it showed up on this page. When I was rude to my mother, it showed up on this page.

At the end of your life, all these pages were added up

and that's what your life was worth. Good, bad. Good, bad. Good, bad. Even with this knowledge, I kept lying about Ray. Bad. While my other friends were out with nice, middle-class Jewish boys, I was out with a guy my parents viewed as an outlaw. He was the first of many outlaws to come.

As I graduated from high school, I had no idea what I wanted to do. I thought, for a time, I wanted to be Tina Turner. Or Dagny Taggart, the woman who ran a railroad in Ayn Rand's *Atlas Shrugged*. They were my only two role models. My mother was sort of one—courageous and gutsy—a business executive at a time when it was rare for women to be in management. But I got mixed signals from her. She never enjoyed her work or felt fulfilled by it. In fact, she felt shame and embarrassment at having to work. She did it out of desperation. It wasn't a career. It was a job.

There were also mixed signals about relationships with men and her role in the marriage, which was as much generational as it was unique to my parents. Although my mother was the major breadwinner for a while, when she had to travel on business, my father wouldn't let her sleep overnight. She always honored him.

So I went to college with no idea of what I was going to do when I grew up. Or why I was really going to college at all. Except that I knew I had to escape my parents.

3

YOU GOTTA DO
WHAT YOU GOTTA DO

1967. THE YEAR OF THE FIRST HEART TRANSPLANT AND THE first microwave oven. Elvis and Priscilla tie the knot in Vegas. The Beatles release "Sgt. Pepper's Lonely Hearts Club Band." The Young Rascals release "Groovin'." Everybody who's not humming "All You Need Is Love" is singing along with the Stones' "Ruby Tuesday." The Monterey Pop Festival draws 50,000 kids. *Batman* is a big hit on TV. The big movies are *The Graduate, Jungle Book, Guess Who's Coming to Dinner, Bonnie and Clyde* and *The Dirty Dozen. Barbarella* is banned by the Church before it even goes into production.

I needed the cash to help pay my tuition at Boston University. So I quietly took a job as a go-go dancer/

waitress in a bar on Commonwealth Avenue—
wearing a fringed miniskirt and fake white Courreges
boots, throwing my hair from left to right like Lada
Edmund, Jr., did on *Hullabaloo* when she did the
frug.

Everyone was busy declaring "majors." So I declared a major in marketing. After all, I'd been terrific
at selling shoes.

I was often the only girl in my classes at the College
of Business Administration at BU. I liked that. I liked
being one of the boys. In fact, it was just about the
only thing I liked about BU.

I felt isolated there. Once again, I didn't have
enough money in an environment where a lot of kids
had too much. I had little in common with my
dormmates; one of whom was stoned twenty-four
hours a day for the whole year I knew her; another
who spent all of her free time with her head on an
ironing board, ironing out her curls. Straight hair was
in. Plus, I wasn't doing well scholastically. I took
calculus twice and flunked it both times.

The isolation at home was more familiar to me than
the isolation at BU. So, after my freshman year, I
transferred to NYU's School of Commerce to continue studying marketing.

I had to live at home, and to help pay tuition I got a
job as an assistant bookkeeper after school. Every
morning I took the bus to the train station in Great
Neck, the train to Penn Station in Manhattan, and the
subway downtown to NYU in Greenwich Village.
After classes, I took the subway back uptown from
NYU to my job, then back to Penn Station and the
train and bus home.

The traveling was tedious, but something happened to me once on my way home which I've never forgotten.

I was just starting up the stairs out of the subway, when someone put his hand under my skirt and grabbed me by the crotch. My first thought was this must be someone I know. Who else would have the nerve? No, it was some creep!

I was carrying an umbrella and I beaned him with it. He fell down the stairs and I ran to the top of the stairs, shaking. I was holding on to the banister to steady myself when a cop who had seen the whole thing walked up to me and said, "Honey, I'm going to give you one lesson. Don't forget it. When you walk down the street, look people in the eye and think: 'Don't fuck with me, fella.'"

He was talking about attitude—the kind of attitude that makes you look so powerful that no one would even think about attacking you or putting you down. It's the look that Mafia boss John Gotti had on his face in all the newspaper clippings, as he strode in and out of courtrooms on trial for racketeering and murder (at least until the last one), it's the game face Michael Jordan wears out on that court, it's the glare a tough street kid uses to get the other kid to keep his gun in his pocket, it's the way Miles Davis stared down his audience, it's the expression Anita Hill wore as she faced the senators' questioning—a kind of visual chutzpah.

We're talking about the kind of attitude you wear like armor. Attitude that helps you dazzle the enemy, dissolve obstacles, and allows you to charge ahead even while you're still cleaning up the mess that's inside.

Attitude came easy for me. Some people are born with it, but if you weren't you can cultivate it. If you're filled with self-doubt, your capacity for attitude may be dormant, but you can develop it. Don't forget, it doesn't have to reflect who you really feel you are. It's a performance. The magic of it is that just doing it turns it into a kind of self-fulfilling prophecy. You get used to it.

In New York, in Washington, in Hollywood and in many other places, perceived power is a kind of power. Once you've scored a few successes with attitude, the reinforcement of your confidence helps the deeper, gut-rooted strength to emerge. Of course, the best kind of attitude is exuded by a person operating not from perceived but from real power—from his or her own internal strengths and his or her consciousness of them. But that will come.

In the meantime, put on your attitude and get out there. Be brilliant. Be successful.

Why be successful? Why not?

I actually got through the psychedelic sixties without ever being into drugs. The business schools were only into ambition. I also missed all the protests. At the time, 10,000 hippies were staging a love-in in Central Park, and a multitude of students were protesting at NYU. I couldn't figure out how these people had time to picket.

While they were marching and protesting, loving-in, turning on and tuning out, I was taking accounting classes and studying inventory methods like LIFO (Last In, First Out) and FIFO (First In, First Out).

At the time, my burning social issues were my own mental survival and whether to elope with my boyfriend, Neil.

Neil Landau was a very handsome gambler, a compulsive gambler, and that really excited me. It was thrilling to go to the Knicks games and sit on the floor, or go to the Rangers games, and to the horse races where all the cashiers actually knew him by name! My boyfriends in high school had liked sports but it's a whole different world when you're into high-stakes betting. We're talking tens of thousands of dollars, and he was twenty years old.

He was the first person I knew who had anything to do with the movie business. His father, Ely Landau, had produced many important movies such as *The Pawnbroker* and *Long Day's Journey into Night*. We would sometimes go to Neil's house in Riverdale on Saturday nights and look at movies. This was the first time I was ever in a private screening room.

But mostly, weekends would find us at the track or at a blackjack table. We went to Las Vegas, to Atlantic City. Once we almost eloped to Elkton, Maryland—where it was legal to marry without a blood test—but stopped on the way at a track called Pimlico, lost all our money and had to come back. On more than one occasion, he gambled away my tuition money and then won it back on the same day. It was always an on-the-edge kind of atmosphere with Neil. I loved it.

I believed I loved him. He was very engaging, as many people with addictive personalities are. And, of course, he was tormented, though I could never figure out how to help him. When we broke up, he came sobbing to my house, where my father, who had never comforted anyone other than his children, comforted Neil.

Then there was Joey, the most important of my boyfriends from the seventies. He was in the music business. He had lots of kids and a wife and he would never leave them. My relationship with him lasted five years. I adored him.

But I kept choosing men I couldn't have. Men I couldn't help, I couldn't save, I couldn't nurture. I went from one masochistic relationship to the next. I was the classic other woman, which is to say, the classic sap: you always dream they'll leave their wife. But they don't. Or they didn't for me.

Why did I do this to myself? Of course, as I later learned, these men were all about my father. As I entered the serious scene in New York, the key figure in my development, or my lack of development, was a self-protective, emotionally closed man—my father.

I was ready for sex, but not ready to be loved. Not ready to be cherished. I had no practice. For many years, I would replicate the basic emotional dynamic of my relationship with my father by choosing unavailable, inappropriate men.

But from Neil I nevertheless learned two useful things. He taught me about the point spread, which would eventually help me in my next job and prepare me for the movie business. I also learned an important lesson about playing the odds: *Be a gambler, but quit before you self-destruct.*

When Neil first took me to Las Vegas I discovered I was a natural gambler. I loved it and was great at it. I could have become a compulsive gambler. But I had a sense of survival. Neil became for me a model both of what to do and of what not to do.

The challenge for me was to find ways to gamble that were not self-destructive. It turns out that there's no better habit to bring to the workplace than risk-taking. You have to gamble if you're going to break out of the pack of conformists and blaze any kind of career trail. Risk-taking makes you an innovator, a leader. Of course, you can lose. My advice is gamble anyway. No risk, no gain. Most of my career has been about finding socially acceptable ways to indulge my habit.

At the time, I was exhausted from the commuting to classes and the after-school work. I still felt like a failure in school and I had run out of money, out of interest, out of patience. But I wasn't ready to find a husband and settle down like a lot of my friends were doing. I wanted a job. I wanted a career.

At least I thought that's what I wanted. I had my doubts about working. My mother had worked. But she didn't have the luxury of fantasizing about a career. She was painfully ambivalent about having to work. And here I was choosing it. The truth is, I had no choice. Someone had to pay my bills.

It took me decades to understand my ambivalence about working.

So, anyway, in 1968, I quit school and got my first full-time job. I combed the want ads in *The New York Times* and found a job agency. This was not a placement firm, not a headhunter—this was an employment agency. My first job was filling in as a receptionist in a garment district company with the unlikely name of Rob Roy. Shortly afterward I changed companies and became the receptionist for a small sports book publisher, the Stadia Publishing Company.

At Stadia, I worked my way up the ladder women know all too well, the ladder that goes from receptionist to secretary and stops right there.

I didn't want to be the receptionist. I wanted to meet the athletes. I wanted to know their stories. I wanted to write their stories. So *I pushed; I put on my helmet and my attitude and I pushed.*

Girls who had played with dolls might have been intimidated working in sports publishing. Not me. This was, in a way, a dream come true for the kid who was out there to make it as a man.

There was no way I could get into the locker room (although, decades later, even that taboo was shattered when women journalists sued and won that right). But at least I was surrounded by men who had been raised there. I could learn some of the stuff they knew. *Guys understand almost from birth about networking and team play and being competitive and not taking it personally if you lose (that one took me a long time).* These are things for which women have been compensating for the last thirty years. We're getting there. We're learning about team play and alliances.

After a couple of months, I convinced the people I worked for that I could do some writing and editing. I started working on books with titles like *The NFL*

Digest and *The Major League Baseball Digest*. My first mentor was Don Smith, who was the public relations director for the New York Giants football team. He was free-lancing on the side for Stadia Publishing. He thought I might be good at sportswriting.

A mentor is invaluable. Find one. Someone who will spot your raw, natural gifts and groom you to do more than you're doing. Someone who has a big mind. Big-minded people don't feel threatened.

What did I know about football? When my brother and I were kids, he had been the tight end on the junior varsity team and, at home, I was the quarterback who helped him practice. I had a pretty mean passing arm and great aim. And from my old boyfriend Neil I knew the point spread.

I got sent to Yankee Stadium to cover a Giants game. When I got there I knocked on the door of the press box, with all my credentials hanging out of my pockets. The door opened, revealing a huge guy with a big red nose with broken red capillaries running through it.

"What do you want, kid?" he asked gruffly.

I said, "I'm Dawn Steel and I'm here to cover the game for *The NFL Digest.*" And I pushed my credentials forward.

He looked back at me without a smile. "You can't come in here," he said.

"Why not?" I asked.

"Because you're a girl."

"Yeah, I know I'm a girl, but why can't I come in here?" I asked.

"No girl's ever been in the Yankee Stadium press box, kid," he announced.

It was the first time in my life that I really came up against the crude and overt exclusion of girls and women. I was stunned, then furious. But rather than slink away with my credentials between my legs, I raised an incredible stink. And they wound up having to make me an auxiliary press box, a turret that hung out, literally, over the fifty-yard line.

Never mind that you had to crawl on all fours through a tunnel to get there. I was in a box. The guys in charge learned that some girls fight back. I learned not to take no for an answer.

As it turned out, every Sunday some very well-known people sat in my box. My little press box became a hip place to be. Among the "alternative" box luminaries were the men who were assigned the color commentary that was broadcast around the play-by-play.

These very cold Sunday mornings produced some very hung-over guys. One Sunday, one particularly hung-over guy shoved the microphone in my face and said, "You can do it. You do the play-by-play."

"Oh, my God, I don't know anything about football," I slipped, undermining my capacity as the ace reporter for the illustrious *NFL Digest*. I didn't have a clue how to begin.

I looked out on the football field. And there were the ugliest purple uniforms I had ever seen. I may not have known about football. But I knew clothes.

I launched into a fashion commentary on the putrid purple uniforms the Vikings were wearing.

People laughed. It was the first time I got real feedback that let me know I was funny. It was an important moment for me. What I learned in that press box is that you can force your voice if you have to.

Once you've done it, remember what it feels like, so that you can call it up in your memory next time you need it. To get the guts to go on the radio, I probably intuitively called up the great feeling of getting into the Kilties and getting the job at the shoe store, my only two previous triumphs. It was a small first step in learning how to give myself approval. But these small steps are what change your life.

I called on it, sometimes desperately, as I took on bigger and bigger challenges. Some of the things that terrified me so much then really don't seem like much now, but I was learning to function. I never got over being painfully shy, but I learned how to compensate for it.

I still remember the feeling of pure dread I had as I walked down the hall of the Waldorf Towers one afternoon to meet one of my heroes, Irwin Shaw. He was the first important writer I'd ever met. He was an author. I was researching a book called *Baseball, The First One Hundred Years,* and one of the things I had to do was compile research for Irwin Shaw, who had been asked to write the introduction called "Before the Pros."

I got a letter from him asking me the following question: What was the world like in 1869—around the time when baseball was born—culturally, musically, politically, in the United States, and all over the world? I read this letter, thinking with a sinking feeling, Oh, my God, this is the most extensive research project I've ever seen. I was overwhelmed. Every night, I went to the public library and sat there, feverishly compiling a research paper that was going to be read by Irwin Shaw. Irwin Shaw! The author of *The Young Lions*. If my father was King of the Giants, this was the King of Words.

As I walked toward Irwin Shaw's door, I felt I'd never be able to carry on a conversation. I got to his door and there was a lion's head knocker and I thought: How incredibly cool! A lion's head knocker for the man who wrote *The Young Lions*. I expected someone like Arthur Miller, who seemed to me to be the prototype of the literary intellectual—a very erudite, smooth, urbane guy, lean and cerebral.

But then Irwin Shaw opened the door. He had a terrible cold and he was bombed. I think he'd been drinking schnapps to clear his nasal passages. Let's just say that this was not a distinguished sight.

And yet even in that state, there still emanated from Shaw something very powerful. It emerged as soon as we began talking about the project: Shaw had passion. It was the first time I'd come into contact with creative passion of such magnitude. This was not a novel that was going to sell a million copies, but his passion for baseball was very intense, a passion he could translate into his work on our project.

Weeks later, his piece was delivered and it opened with something like "The year was 1869 and there was a president called Johnson who was in trouble then, too."

Hmmm, this all sounds very familiar, I thought.

He'd written the words "By Irwin Shaw." But as I read on, it was all, verbatim, my research. I was moved and thrilled that Irwin Shaw had used my research. I was flattered to death that he had plagiarized me!

After all, in my perception, he was a celebrity and I was just some schlepper.

There is a lesson about how your confidence level changes your perception. And about how your awe can be misguiding. Years later, I was back in the hallway of the Waldorf Towers and I noticed that the whole hallway—every door, not just Irwin Shaw's— had a lion's head knocker. Was I a schmuck or what?

Many New York newspapers had gone out of business or were on their way out. The *Herald Tribune* went first. Then the *Telegram*. Then the *Journal American*. A lot of experienced, male sportswriters were out of work. And here I was, a female, working for $125 a week. There was pressure, and it was time for a new job.

A friend told me about a job at a new magazine no one had heard of yet called *Penthouse*. It was an English magazine that was about to be launched in America. This was not *The New York Review of Books*. It was a girly magazine. I interviewed and got the job. I said good-bye to my Yankee Stadium press box and told my parents I was going to work for *Mademoiselle* magazine.

4

GOOD-BYE, GOOD LUCK AND BREAK A LEG

1969. RICHARD NIXON IS SWORN IN AS PRESIDENT. PHILIP Roth publishes *Portnoy's Complaint*. CBS kills *The Smothers Brothers* show, which it sees as too controversial. The first live color TV coverage of the moon is seen on earth. *Butch Cassidy and the Sundance Kid, The Love Bug, Midnight Cowboy, Easy Rider* and *Hello Dolly* must compete for America's attention with the Sharon Tate Murder and Woodstock. *Hair* hits big. "Aquarius/Let the Sun Shine In" is the number-one song, closely followed by "Sugar, Sugar," by the Archies, "Honky Tonk Women," by the Rolling Stones and "Come Together," by the Beatles.

Around the time ten thousand women marched down Fifth Avenue with Betty Friedan, Gloria Steinem and Bella Abzug to celebrate fifty years of voting and to demand day care, equal pay and promotions, and nonsexist advertising, I went to work for *Penthouse*. I was joining a publication at which I would make my mark creating overtly sexist advertising and selling hand-knit "Cock Socks," a publication which was building its four-and-a-half-million circulation on bare breasts, while, a few blocks away, Gloria Steinem and friends were preparing to start *Ms.* magazine.

I didn't know Gloria Steinem then. I didn't know any feminists. I was not a member of the literati, which I believed these women came from, this highly articulate group of women who had found their voices. Steinem had gone to Smith. How could I know her?

I didn't understand what the women's movement was about. It wasn't that I was unaware of discrimination—I simply never felt it. Apart from the incident over the press box that ended satisfactorily, I never felt discriminated against. I think that even then I had a personality that discouraged harassment. If there was sexism at *Penthouse,* I didn't notice it. Or maybe I didn't permit it. Because I was not afraid of men, I stood up to them.

But let's face it, I was working for a publisher condemned by many as a notorious exploiter of women, Bob Guccione. How could I work there?

One reason was that there was a climate of liberation. In a way, working for *Penthouse* was a very liberated action for a young woman from a lower-middle-class family. You had to have a lot of nerve to go to work for *Penthouse* in the first place, and I already had that. To a great extent, *Penthouse* was perfect for me because it was the locker room. Finally, I was one of the guys, or as close to it as I could come.

The second factor is that Guccione's product may have been demeaning to women but he himself was not. Toward me, he behaved impeccably. We did not have a sexual relationship. Yet he was the most sensual man I'd ever seen. He walked into a room and radiated sex. But he wasn't interested in me and I wasn't having fantasies about him; I learned the lesson that you could have a wonderful working relationship with an attractive man and not want to sleep with him.

Bob Guccione was not sexist. In terms of work, he certainly believed in women. He promoted me over and over again. Many of his senior positions were filled by very strong, highly intelligent women, not the least of whom was Kathy Keeton, later to become his wife, who was really the publisher of the magazine. Two other of his employees are among my oldest friends. One of them was Gay Bryant, now editor-in-chief of *Mirabella* magazine. Another was Beverley Wardale, who's still at *Penthouse* as senior vice president and corporate director for advertising and marketing in the U.K. and Europe. The women who worked their way up in Bob Guccione's company found that the ladder did not end at the secretarial pool. Bob supported women's rights and women's right to choice long before it was fashionable to do so.

Guccione was a multifaceted man. He had a staggering art collection in his home, something I had previously seen only in museums. He had a huge, very close Italian family and I was a part of that family. I'm very grateful to Bob Guccione.

* * *

But I must have had conflicting feelings—because even while I insisted to myself and my friends that I was not embarrassed by the job, I did lie to my parents and tell them I was working for *Mademoiselle*. I saw that at the time as an appropriate white lie. And I still think that, although I wish there hadn't been the necessity for it. I knew that my working for this racy magazine would embarrass my parents. When my mother's friends would ask, "What's Dawn doing, Lillian?" She'd have to say, "She's working for a smut magazine. . . ."

There's no doubt that *Penthouse* was a fantastic opportunity for me. Because it was a new magazine, everyone did everything. I was the receptionist, the secretary, the articles editor for a few seconds, a fiction editor, and then the travel editor. I was in Chile the day Allende was shot. I was happening.

During my minute as an interviewer, Orson Welles taught me a very humiliating but useful lesson: *Do your homework*. I'd been sent to get an interview with Welles, my first big assignment. I did research and I prepared—I hadn't been a film buff but I read everything I could find about him, and worked for a long time on writing him a really impressive letter that began, *"Dear Mr. Wells . . ."*

He sent back a scathing answer to my request for an interview, saying, "Why would I give an interview to someone who can't even spell my name right?" I had done all that homework and spelled his name wrong. I never made that mistake again—ever. And I've become as tough as Orson Welles. When job applicants send me résumés addressed to *Mr. Don Steele*—which they do, all the time—I invariably throw their letters in the wastebasket.

But the larger lesson is about taking whatever job you do seriously and doing it better than everyone else. Any task is an expression of your standards and your personality. You bring dignity to the job.

It also helped, at *Penthouse,* not to look like a "Pet." How you dress is essential to the image you project and to your own dignity. Your clothes are a reflection of how you see yourself.

I learned from my mother how to dress and she gave me this advice when I started dressing for work: *"Buy just one good, classic thing a year.* Less is more."

My mother had great taste. She had a sense of style in the way she dressed and how she decorated. And she had style without money. People commented on it all the time. Where did she learn it? Not at home, because Grandma had zero style. She was a Russian immigrant who wore cheap cotton muumuu housedresses. Who spent money on clothes?

But my mother used to tell me that it's much more important to go out wearing a simple black dress and strand of fake pearls than it is to buy twenty different things that will look ridiculous in two weeks. When I started working, I wore a very, very simple black suit. You couldn't tell it was cheap. I never wore jewelry. Just a watch. That was it.

I still had a terrible body image. I remember feeling thrilled and disbelieving when a line in an article about me said, "If things get bad at *Penthouse,* Dawn will have no trouble getting a job as a high-fashion model." Who were they talking about? That certainly did not match my view of myself. But, somehow, intuitively, I was arriving at a look that worked for me. My own style was emerging.

That article also showed me that I had something

going for me in my name. The headline and the lead paragraph made the joke about my name sounding like a nightclub stripper. It made colorful copy, and that was okay by me. *The thing is, you do have to get their attention. Use what you've got.*

By the time the story appeared, I was *Penthouse*'s merchandise editor. That title was a reward for starting something now called "advertorials." I'd write editorials about cameras or stereos or luggage, and then the ad department sold ads to the industry I wrote about. They were successful and they got Guccione's attention.

One day he called me up and said, "Congratulations, I'm making you head of merchandising."

"What's that mean?" I asked.

"Good-bye, good luck, break a leg," he said. And hung up.

I didn't really know what merchandising was. As it turned out my job was to start two divisions. One of them was setting up a licensing operation like *Playboy*'s, to license our logo to sell pajamas, underwear, belts and so forth. The other was a mail-order division set up to sell inexpensive off-color gifts.

The article with my picture showed one of my advertorials. It was an article about men's underwear. My idea for the ad had been to use a famous etching by Albrecht Dürer of Adam and Eve in the Garden of Eden. I had a set built that looked like the etching, had models pose as Adam and Eve in exactly the same way as in the etching, with Eve in a fig leaf and Adam wearing jockey shorts. The copy read: "Introducing the 1973 Fig Leaf."

When I look back on it, I know it was good work. It

was not distasteful, yet it was very sexy and provocative. It was the beginning of a very productive period for me, when I really came into my own as an idea person.

I had no idea where all this stuff came from in my mind. I knew I had a thousand crazy ideas, that I could smell a successful product and just sort of know what the market wanted. I didn't think of this as a talent. To me, talents were singing or painting or acting. I was doing well in marketing but, to me, selling was not a gift. In my family, selling was always considered an act of desperation.

What Bob Guccione did for me, what he managed to urge out of me by giving me one challenge after another, was what I know to be the biggest gift of all: my instincts. When I recently reread that article, I laughed. It says: " 'It doesn't take much of an investment to start a licensing operation,' Miss Steel explained. 'It's not like I have to stock an inventory.' " God, it sounds like I knew what I was doing!

But I also hear something in that arrogant quote that tells me I was beginning to follow my instincts as an entrepreneur. I was becoming a risk-taker. Even though I was still almost pathologically insecure, I was beginning to follow my nose.

In my new job, I committed myself, body and soul, to finding the greatest "slightly off-color" products in the world. I searched long and hard, from New York to Munich to Hong Kong to Paris. In Frankfurt, on one of my buying trips, I finally found myself in, of all places, Dr. Meuller's Sex Shop. And I found the ultimate gift for the man who read *Penthouse:* the COCK SOCK.

I couldn't wait to share them with the world. In fact, I remember, right after I got home, being in a cab with my girlfriend Margie and pulling one out of my purse.

"What do you think?" I said to Margie.

She looked at this hand-knit, pastel-colored thing, and said, "It looks like a baby mitten. What is it?"

"It's a Cock Sock!"

"A what?" Margie asked.

"A Cock Sock," I said proudly. "I'm going to rename it."

"To what?" she asked tentatively.

"A banana warmer," I answered enthusiastically. "Is this great or what! Women knitted them during World War Two for their husbands."

Margie, who was shocked to the point of catatonia, managed to say, "Dawn, I have to say I've never seen anything like it."

A perfect thing to say, grist for my mill. Because by now I had lost my inhibitions not only about sex-related merchandise, but also about merchandising itself. I could already see the promotion, a picture of a sexy, naked woman, holding up a sock. "For the man who has everything and nowhere to put it."

And that's exactly what the ad became. I had the socks manufactured in the very patriotic colors red, white and blue.

I marked them all extra large.

5

GROW
YOUR OWN
PENIS

1972. RICHARD NIXON WINS A SECOND TERM BY A LAND-slide. America's heart belongs to young Soviet gymnast Olga Korbut, who cleans up on Olympic gold medals. Right around here the fitness craze is born. The big movies are *The Godfather; The Poseidon Adventure; What's Up, Doc?; Deliverance;* and *Jeremiah Johnson.* The hit songs are "American Pie," "Heart of Gold," "The First Time Ever I Saw Your Face," "I Can See Clearly Now" and Helen Reddy's "I Am Woman."

I had a ball in my *Penthouse* days. The fact that I was having an affair with a married man left me free a good deal of the time. This was the early seventies, when Manhattan was booming socially. *Penthouse* introduced me to the world of British and Australian journalists who free-lanced for the magazine. I loved to hang out with them at Costello's, a bar on Third Avenue in New York, and listen to their stories. I had many gay friends, too, and we'd go out dancing till late in the night. This was the height of the disco era. I truly had a Saturday Night Fever.

For me and for millions of other young, single people, it was an era of experiments of all sorts. I still wasn't into drugs, though once, around that time, I smoked some marijuana at a party.

I was convinced that it had no effect on me whatsoever. I kept saying, "What's the big deal? What does it feel like to be stoned? I'm not stoned."

Except that I'd become obsessed with the record player. I couldn't take my eyes off the record as it circled around and around and around.

I walked over to the record player. I bent down to get a better view of the spinning disc. Way down. And caught my lip in the needle.

I didn't move, afraid that someone would see my lip stuck in the stylus. Finally, my brother wandered over to see what his big sister was doing with her head on the record.

"Help me," I managed to whisper. And then, "Very carefully."

My brother was awed. He gently extricated my lower lip from the needle. It was bleeding.

"You're an asshole," he said.

I concurred. And I never smoked grass again.

Other experiments were more fruitful. I took a course called "Mind Dimensions and Control." Several hundred people attended these weekend conferences where you were supposed to learn to take control of your own mind and your life. They were usually held in hotels.

The course taught you how to create pictures of yourself in any situation you desired. So that if you were unhappy and you wanted to visualize yourself happy, it taught you how to rummage through your own image bank to come up with effective mental pictures.

I loved learning that technique and it actually provoked a big change in my inner life. I've long forgotten some of the other "Mind Dimensions and Control" instructions, but I never stopped using the visualizations. *Every success I've had I've visualized beforehand.* In those New York days, when I hadn't had a chance to have much success, there was plenty of material to work with. I was filled with dreams of achievement and romance and the difference between the hopes and the realities often loomed very large, so this was progress for me.

And now I moved ahead on another front. I made my first really close woman friend, Margic Glucksman—the first woman I ever trusted. Margie was a theatrical agent, booking actors for commercials. She was from Brooklyn, and was two years younger than I was. When we met in the spring of 1973, I was a basket case because I had just broken up the week before with Joey, my married man. I still adored him, and I would for years, but five years was enough.

I met Margie at a party one night at Todd Finkel's, an old high school friend of mine who went on to own a shoe store on Third Avenue, Vittorio Ricci. (My memory is terrible, but ask me about shoes and I remember anything and everything.)

I said to Margie, "Let's have brunch Sunday." I had an ulterior motive. I wanted her to come with me to Central Park, where one of Joey's rock acts was having a concert. Joey was a rock 'n' roll record producer.

I just wanted to gaze at him. One last time.

It was a mob scene at the Sheep Meadow. We snuck in backstage, sweating bullets. But we couldn't see him. I felt like an idiot. Only someone as driven by lovesickness as I was could have had such bad judgment. It was one of these outings that seemed like a good plan when it was conceived and just fizzled out into this terrible afternoon. Margie was just great about it. I couldn't believe that someone I had just met had gone through all this with a stranger and that this woman who didn't know me had endured this craziness with no editorial comments. Margie was the first person in my life since my grandparents who was completely accepting and nonjudgmental. Over lunch that day at a restaurant called Central Park, I laid it out. "I want you to know this," I announced. "I don't have women friends."

We were best friends from that day on. We had a wonderful time together. We loved to shop on Orchard Street on Sundays on the Lower East Side of Manhattan. We went to San Juan and St. Thomas together. We went to Elaine's and the Apollo in Harlem. We gossiped about whether Chevy Chase would really call Margie after she had run into him in the lobby of my apartment building and he'd asked for her number. He never did.

Mind you, by now we're in the seventies, the high

drama of *Roe* v. *Wade,* massive opposition to U.S. involvement in Vietnam, Watergate and the resignation of Richard Nixon.

Margie and I shared the same uninvolvement in politics, feminism and human rights. We were unaware together. We were literally the girl in *Working Girl.* We would get on the bus in the morning, we'd go to work.

Yet we were creatures of our era, in ways we didn't understand then. We were split in half. One half of us was looking for rich husbands to take care of us. The other half was looking for careers and independence. Both of us were doing well. We loved it. We were making our own money, we could buy clothes and take vacations. Our conflicts really showed in the men we chose, men we couldn't marry, men who would never put our conflicts between marriage and a career to the test. Margie, like me, had a long impossible relationship with an unavailable man.

Why didn't we think of combining career and a husband? It was hard to figure out how to do it, unless you did it like my mother had done, out of necessity. But if you found your work thrilling and were really engaged by its challenges and your future in it, there were very few role models. And because our parents didn't really approve of what we were doing (even while they were proud of us, they still thought we'd be better off with nice, rich husbands), here we were on this new adventure for women, with virtually no support behind us.

Our peers were not much more help. There were very few women out there doing what we were doing. At William Morris, where Margie had worked, even the secretaries were men. We had risen above secretaries, but who knew how far we would go? Who was there to advise us?

We lived for Joel Egan to read our palms and tell us our destiny. Joel was a plump, pear-shaped, very sweet actor with an extraordinary psychic ability. He was gay and camp and outrageous and very funny and he was our best friend. He had been born with a congenital heart defect and always knew he would die young. He did. That may have heightened his insights. In our palms, he saw our men, our babies, our careers. He was always right. He predicted I'd have a daughter and he predicted the initials of my first husband, R.R.R.

He saw California in my palm. He was reading my palm one day and said, "Dawn, you're going to leave New York and move to Los Angeles."

"I don't know anyone in Los Angeles," I said.

"You're going to Hollywood," he said.

"Please, I don't know how to sing, dance or act."

"You're gonna be a star," he insisted.

I thought Joel must be having an off day.

Margie and I were addicted to Joel. He played with our lives and we loved it.

Joel was also a creature of his era. For instance, he wore makeup a lot of the time. You might say he had an interesting interpretation of gender stereotypes. If the new breed of ambitious young women were terrifying to men, they did not frighten Joel, who had been raised by a strong mother and a strong sister. Joel loved us and we loved him. We validated each other in a threatened and unforgiving macho world.

Aside from marriage, some other time-honored alternatives presented themselves. Being a kept woman was something I didn't seriously consider, but I had offers.

I had met a man on a plane going to the Chicago Gift Fair. When we landed, there was a harrowing blizzard and no cabs.

But there was this white Rolls-Royce. It was waiting for the man from the plane, a schlepp in a polyester suit with pens stuck in his shirt. He asked if he could give me a lift. I kept hearing my mother's voice—Don't take rides from strangers—as I let him drive me to the hotel. As he dropped me off, he said, "I'd like to see you again." At dinner that night, he offered to buy me a coop, furnish it, and take care of me.

I can't take much credit for turning him down. He wasn't hard to refuse. He was fat. He had greased-back black hair and a curlicue waxed moustache. No kidding.

And yet I knew women who thought differently. My friend Linda, for instance. I met her in my exercise class on Fifty-seventh Street. It was right after I'd broken up with Joey, and I often sat in this class doing my stretches, tears rolling down my face. "Is it that painful, this class?" asked a gorgeous, tall brunette with a great skinny body and big boobs who was sitting right next to me. We became friends.

I believe Linda introduced Margie and me to every rich man in town. Some of the scenes were amazing and could have happened only in Manhattan in those days. I remember one night her limo picked me up for drinks at The Pierre hotel and dinner at Elaine's with what turned out to be a Middle Eastern prince, an Arab and several Israelis. I sat there thinking, Oh, my God, they're going to kill each other. And when they didn't, I decided there must be hope for the world.

Linda was an innocent, a true Holly Golightly character. She was the most generous person I had ever met. She shared everything, her men, her clothes, her friends. She was not threatened by other women and was always looking for wonderful women to join her crowd. She didn't work, as far as I could see. She lived in the George Cinq on Fifth Avenue in a gorgeous apartment filled with spectacular antiques.

We never asked if she was a hooker and she never told us. But Margie and I would ask each other how she could live like this with no visible means of support. Who paid the rent? How was it she was always free for lunch, looking fabulous with her nails and hair just done? We were told she was kept by the biggest real estate developer in New York City. "She's half a hooker," I would say to Margie, in an attempt to rationalize. It was a dilemma typical of the times when the parameters of all the traditional categories had become extremely fuzzy.

I was very proud of myself for having earned my first mink coat all by myself. It was made by Linda's furrier. Who knew from furriers? It was very dark, Blackglama mink—you know, the "What Becomes a Legend Most?" mink. It had a hood lined with black velvet. That hood to me was Julie Christie in *Doctor Zhivago*.

This was 1972, and the movie of the year was Francis Ford Coppola's *The Godfather,* which, though I didn't know it then, launched a revolution in Hollywood in which I would eventually find myself. *The Godfather* showed young filmmakers that a quality movie could also be a commercial success. It spurred brilliant and idealistic young people from film school and the entertainment industry in New York to go out to Hollywood to make movies and change the world. The exodus from New York to Hollywood began around this time.

But I was more drawn to *Doctor Zhivago,* which came out the year I moved to the city. I loved David Lean for making it. It was the romance that swept me away. All this passion and white fur and sparkling snow crystals was not exactly the Russia my family had told me about. This incredible, tragic love that endured revolutions and snowdrifts was not my schleppy affairs with gamblers and married men. I wanted to be Lara. With the hood, it was as close as I could get to Julie Christie.

Money was now coming in from two sources. I was still head of merchandising at *Penthouse.* But the entrepreneuring bug had bitten me and I started my own little mail-order company on the side. I was hunting, now, for products for my own company, operating out of my apartment, which was getting to look like a shipping room.

To Margie, I had a magic touch with money. Margie's father was out of work so she was helping her parents and had very little money. But she had a loving family.

I always envied her family. She envied me my hair and my clothes. So we traded.

Margie and I talked about those days recently, and she reminded me that I was always giving her stuff. At the time, I used to wear gray flannel pants and blazers and silk shirts in a zillion colors that I'd buy cheap on Orchard Street. When I'd go down there I'd pick up some for Margie, too. I gave her luggage when she moved to California and sheets and good cooking pots when she moved into a new place. I also gave Margie my obsession with the latest fads, whether she liked it or not. If I went on a bee pollen, kelp and lecithin diet, so did she. Bikini wax? She had to do it, too. Margie remembers those days fondly. She says I also gave her a little attitude. "I remember a phrase you'd always say to me before I went out," says Margie. "You'd say, 'Go out there. Knock 'em dead!'"

My close friendship with Margie gave me a chance to give in a way I hadn't been able to with all those unavailable men.

But I took, too. Emotionally, I was very needy. Margie gave me something far more valuable than things. I borrowed her family. Margie's family was close and loving and, like her, completely nonjudgmental. Margie went home on weekends all the time and I loved to go with her.

It was a wonderful friendship. I still remember the week Margie and I went to Puerto Rico and talked for one whole day under the palms, one of our great talks about our families and our hopes and fears. I could talk to her about my parents.

Was I depressed? Yes, I was. Big time. But only deep under the surface. I had been in the black hole since my father got sick but I was learning how to function in spite of it. I was able to have fun and sometimes even to forget. Or perhaps to deny. I think I kept my childhood depression all along, but I had put a lid on it. I became a functional depressive. I didn't know I was depressed. I just knew I was missing something. Happy? Who said anything about happy?

* * *

That's why I hooked up with Ronald Richard Rothstein, whom I met through a mutual friend and who became my first husband. Ronnie paid attention to me and made me feel special. He was generous with me the way no one else had ever been. He took me to Wimbledon to see the tennis. For my thirtieth birthday, he gave me a surprise party at Elaine's, the "in" place. There were fortune tellers, every friend I had, and all-night partying.

The next day he gave me a Raggedy Ann doll. *He's giving me a fucking doll for my birthday!* I thought. *He knows I hate dolls.* Then I noticed that it had diamond stud earrings stuck in its ears.

He was handsome and big-chested like my father, and huggy and affectionate like him. Under the rage, I still adored my father.

Going out with Ronnie gave me a chance to do many things I'd never done before. He had been on the University of Pennsylvania tennis team and he taught me tennis.

When I first met him, Ronnie was in the financial investment business. He was an entrepreneur in his own right and came from a family of entrepreneurs: his father had launched the Eden Roc Hotel in Miami Beach.

We started living together and soon started doing business together. I still had my little business going and now we gave it a name. Entrepreneuse Enterprises, Inc. We were always on the lookout for new ideas that we could market. What we were looking for were ideas that I could try at *Penthouse* and if they worked well and made money for *Penthouse* I could then also branch out to other magazines' mail-order sections on behalf of Entrepreneuse Enterprises.

We were living in my rent-controlled, two-room apartment on East Thirty-fifth street. One day, I came home convinced that I had just seen the ultimate product. An amaryllis plant. It was just about to bloom, and as I looked at it I thought, This looks like a penis. It looks just like a penis!

We found a Dutch bulb importer to whom we did not feel the need to confide that we intended to sell amaryllis as Penis Plants. Our product did not exactly have the respectability of tulips.

Ronnie and I put up our own money—we only had a couple of thousand dollars between us—but we convinced people to give us credit. We'd go to the banks and get loans of $5,000 here, $5,000 there. I was twenty-nine and Ronnie was thirty-three and it was a big deal for us. We were learning to take out loans. We were learning to pay them back.

The idea was to make this a mail-order item. We needed an ad. I dreamed up a headline: "Grow Your Own Penis. All it takes is $6.98 and a lot of love." We drew an amaryllis and made it look even more phallic than it was.

My *Penthouse* job was incredibly demanding and the Penis Plants business was driving me crazy with work. I thrived on twenty-hour workdays but this was getting ridiculous. Around that time, I had to go on one of my buying trips to Europe to scout products for *Penthouse*. I was wandering around Dr. Meuller's Sex Shop again and suddenly, standing right in front of a huge display of dildos, I said to myself, What are you doing, Dawn? They're not paying you enough to do this.

That was literally and figuratively true. I discovered that my counterpart at *Playboy* was earning twice my salary. My mail-order enterprise for *Penthouse* was very successful. In fact, it was so successful that I thought I was certainly entitled to make more money, either as a bonus or from a percentage of sales. Fair's fair. Pay me or lose me, Mr. Guccione. So I decided to go to him to ask for a piece of the pie, or some sort of bonus. I talked to my mother about it and she said, "Ask for a percentage of the gross. Not the net. The gross." I was scared, of course. But I called up the memory of the day I demanded my own press box at Yankee Stadium.

I went to see Guccione and I said, "The mail-order division I started for you has become very successful and I would like a percentage of the gross profits."

"You're right," he said to me. "You've been successful. Let me think about it and I'll call you in a couple of days."

The *Penthouse* accountant called me back the next day and said, "According to our calculations you owe us a hundred twenty-five thousand dollars."

This was my first tough introduction to the real-life difference between net and gross. Even though the profits had been huge, the *Penthouse* accounting somehow wound up showing that the expenses came out to be much larger than the revenues. There's a great line David Mamet used in his play, *Speed-the-Plow*. "There is no net." It was a joke about the movie business. But it's no joke. And it applies to every business. I learned that lesson—that there is no net—right then and there and it has served me well everywhere.

Penthouse had gone over the accounts of every single transaction, and had hit me with every bogus expense there was.

71

Gamblers know there's a time to fold. So I folded.

And that's an important lesson: *Know when to cut your losses.*

I had cut the tethering strings. I was out there, ready to launch Penis Plants on an unsuspecting world. We ran an ad in every men's magazine in the country— *Gallery, Penthouse, Hustler.* They were something called Per Inquiry ads, which cost us nothing. We split the take with the magazine.

Within ninety days in the market our Penis Plant was a sensation. Every day a pile of checks arrived at the apartment. You may recall our ad informed the potential customer that all that was required was "$6.98 and a lot of love." We sold 100,000 at a cost to us of 30 cents each.

You figure it out.

I wasn't rich, but even with splitting the take, my expenses and Ronnie's cut, I was beginning to earn into the six figures.

But the best part of Penis Plants was the fun we had. We got letters from all over the world saying things like "What do I do now? My penis wilted." (I didn't want to imagine what our customers were actually doing with this product. . . .)

On New Year's Eve, 1975, Ronnie and I got married. Looking back, I see that I sleepwalked through one of the most important events in my life. But I now see that I was on a certain journey and that marrying Ronnie was part of the path I had to take. And it could have been a lot worse, believe me.

But it was a marriage rooted in Penis Plants, not

made in heaven. I can see why I married Ronnie. He was sweet. He was funny. We were in business together. We brainstormed well. We had a lot of laughs. I loved him and I thought he cherished me, the first man who did. I still wasn't ready to be cherished but I was thirty. An old maid. My father was bugging the hell out of me to get married. So I decided to marry Ronnie and get it over with.

Maybe I should have known from our wedding that this would not be the marriage of my dreams. Both of our parents were in Miami, and because of an awful Eastern Airlines crash, the airport was closed. We had decided to get married on New Year's Eve—for reasons which I can no longer recall. You try to find a rabbi on New Year's Eve. They were all in Miami, too. So we looked in the Yellow Pages, and we found a synagogue on Thirty-first Street and Park Avenue. Sounded very fancy—or verrah fency, as my grandmother would have said. More importantly, it was open.

It was a glorious day, the sun was shining so brightly we decided to walk to temple. As we turned the corner from Park Avenue onto Thirty-first Street—the entrance was on Thirty-first—we saw it, the only tenement on the block. It had two dead trees in front, not a good sign.

There was a guy standing outside who had a blond Afro, mismatched shoes and socks, who looked like a bum. It was my brother.

Both of our brothers had agreed to be our witnesses. The rabbi showed up an hour late, took one look at our group and announced that brothers could not be witnesses in an Orthodox ceremony. First I heard of Orthodox. So what were we to do?

The rabbi said he knew of nice girls who worked next door and he left to ask them to our wedding. Minutes later he was back with two women who were clearly hookers. I promise you, he didn't know what they did for a living.

The ceremony began. Our two brothers and the hookers grabbed the *chuppa,* which was a rug with four sticks hanging from its corners. In the middle of the ceremony one hooker got so nervous that she dropped the *chuppa* on our heads.

The whole thing was in Hebrew. I didn't understand much, but I did manage to figure out that the rabbi asked my soon-to-be husband if he took this woman to be his lawful wedded wife and that Ronnie acquiesced. And I waited . . . and waited . . . and waited for him to ask me if I took my husband, blah, blah, blah. He never did. So when the ceremony was over, I asked him why he hadn't asked me if I took my husband-to-be, and he deigned to answer, with great condescension, that it didn't matter what the woman said. It only mattered that the man was getting married.

That marriage lasted ten months.

The day after my wedding, we were back at work on Penis Plants. I knew I was in trouble with the marriage right away when I'd introduce myself to people by telling them, "Hi, I'm Dawn Rothstein," which I couldn't do without spitting.

But our marriage did produce one amazing offspring: a brilliant marketing idea which did delay and complicate our breakup. I guess business is one of the ties that bind.

We were always looking for new ideas. A few months after our wedding, we were in Miami at a meeting in a lawyer's office. A Miami babe walked in. She was wearing Gucci. I mean, she was wearing everything Gucci. Gucci scarf, Gucci shoes, Gucci handbag, bracelet, earrings, watch, blouse. The Gucci symbols, the two little letter *G*'s were all over her.

We left the meeting and went to our car. I looked at Ronnie.

"Did you see that woman? She was totally *G*'d out. Is there anything in the world that doesn't have those *G*'s on it?"

Ronnie looked at me. I will never forget the two little words that simultaneously came out of our mouths.

"Toilet paper!" we said.

It was our next product.

6

THE GREAT GUCCI
TOILET PAPER
CAPER

1975. ALL OF AMERICA IS NOW SOLIDLY ADDICTED TO television, despite the end of the favorite national spectacle: the Watergate hearings. Bruce Springsteen's New Jersey street-smart style hits the top forty with "Born to Run." This is the year of *One Flew Over the Cuckoo's Nest, The Rocky Horror Picture Show, Shampoo* and *Dog Day Afternoon.* Audiences scream in the theaters where *Jaws* is shown.

My biggest concern in 1975 was getting my toilet paper project rolling, so to speak. We did our homework and researched the potential legal problems. There were Gucci rip-offs all over the place. No one was being sued. Certainly, Gucci had no interest in producing its own toilet paper. We went to a top trademark lawyer and he said, "You're taking a chance. They may come after you. But what you're doing is a parody that's not hurting Gucci. It's not a rip-off." That was our thinking: our creation was more an homage than a rip-off. As far as we were concerned, the risks were worth taking. And we would not make it under the name Gucci. It would be called Designer Toilet Paper. This was the year after the Pet Rock.

I began work on the design for the wrapping and the pattern. I figured out how to get the red and green stripe on, and the *GC*'s. It was really a *G* and *C* instead of two *G*'s, but when you're tearing off toilet paper, who stops to look closely? It looked great.

We hunted for someone to print it and discovered a hole in the American consumer market. There was no printed toilet paper. It had not been invented yet on a mass market basis. Only one mill was doing it in a small way, an upstate New York paper mill called Stevens and Thompson, a subsidiary of the company that made Frito-Lay wrappers. Stevens did regular toilet paper but he also did dollar bills on toilet paper. This was the only place that could print our Gucci. I convinced this guy in Rochester to manufacture the toilet paper for me. He didn't know who or what Gucci was. He didn't know from rip-offs or parodies, and certainly not from homages.

Unfortunately, as the toilet paper project came together, my marriage fell apart. We both knew we should have been business partners, not marriage partners. Almost from day one of our marriage, Ronnie and I stopped getting along. He loved me, but I didn't value myself as a woman; how could I let him value me? He was such a sweet, good guy and I simply wasn't ready for one.

I got pregnant that spring, and I was profoundly sad

about it. I knew I couldn't have the baby because the marriage was clearly not going to last.

I had an abortion. It was legal. *Roe* v. *Wade* had won us that right two years earlier. I was, and am, passionately pro-choice, but it was a terrible decision to have to make. I'm not sorry I did it but I will always be sorry that I had to do it. It still haunts me and always will.

For me, it was more an emotional than a moral issue. We had planned it for weeks and I thought I was clearheaded. But when I got to the hospital I started sobbing. Uncontrollable sobs. It was the most painful moment of my life.

Ronnie and I still liked each other. We were good business partners and, with some stormy patches, we would continue to be. But we knew we couldn't stay married. By November we were separated. As the new year began I was deeper in my black hole than I had ever been.

Now I knew I was depressed.

Then I saw the movie that changed my life. It changed it both short-term, because it cheered me up so much, and long-term, because it became a model for me of what a movie could do. This was 1976, and the movie was *Rocky*.

It was that inarticulate boxer who gave me the guts and the heart to start scrambling out of my black hole. Forget Sylvester Stallone as Rambo. He will always be Rocky to me, this stumbling, big guy, unconscious of his great heart and power, who put his head down and doggedly fought his way to his dream. He never gave up. When he found his gift and began to believe in it, he found his voice. His fists were his voice, his dignity, his self-confidence.

When he said, "I just want to go the distance," I identified with him completely. The moment he ran up those steps in triumph, arms raised in victory, I wanted it to be me on those steps. I was weeping so much that I couldn't see the screen. At last, I had a role model. Not a male model or a female model, a universal model for a schlepper with dreams.

I was so moved by this movie, so inspired by it, that it got me thinking about movies, and how extraordinary it is that films can make people feel such powerful emotions in a dark movie theater. A movie can change people's feelings about themselves and compel them to go after their dreams. How great it would be, I felt, to make movies that could do that. It occurred to me, for the first time, to think of going to Hollywood. I didn't know then that it was anything more than just another fantasy. But, in fact, *Rocky* would mark me forever and in one way or another I have been remaking *Rocky* for my whole career.

I had a long way to go. My life felt as low as Rocky's in the first scenes. After Ronnie, I felt such remorse. As always, I blamed myself. On some level, it was my fault my father was unresponsive. It was my fault that my mother withheld approval. It was my fault that my marriage hadn't worked. It was my fault, my fault, my fault.

One of my friends used to say, "Dawn apologizes more than anyone I know." That's what you do when you are always feeling that everything is your fault. I'm sorry, I'm sorry. There is a balance you have to find between taking responsibility for your life and blaming yourself for everything that goes wrong in the world. That kind of blame doesn't strengthen your character, it just fuels your self-hate. After Rocky, I was determined to get out of my hole. But I didn't know how. I had tenacity but, somehow, I knew I couldn't do it alone. I needed help. I found a shrink.

"Dr. Levine, help me. My life is, literally, flushing down the john. I have failed in my marriage. I have huge sorrow about my abortion. I always choose the wrong men. I have affairs with married men who will never leave their wives. I date guys who date models, so I date male models, partly to show the guys, and partly to have their beauty reflect on me so I'll feel better about myself. But we walk down the street and everybody stares at the guy I am with, never at me. Then I feel worse. I can't bear dealing with my family. I am clearly incapable of a healthy relationship. What's wrong with me?" I poured it all out to my first psychiatrist, Dr. David Levine.

I was dysfunctional, as was my family. We use the word "dysfunctional" all the time now, and it is a perfectly good word. But it has become part of a New Age psycho-jargon that sanitizes the kind of crude pain I felt at the time. I did not need a word with a Greek prefix to know I was screwed up and hurt like hell. I just wanted to get fixed.

I had no problem going to a therapist. I have never had a problem taking what I needed to learn from wherever I could find it, and sponging it up. I always had a nose for going to the best sources, the best mentors. I still do, and I advise everyone to do so. *Get whatever help you need. Get yourself a mentor. Fast.*

This makes me a great consumer of help, wherever I find it. Whether it's Dr. Meuller's Sex Shop, whether it's a girlfriend to scrape me up off the floor after some catastrophe, whether it's psychics, exercise classes, a New Age book, a fifty-mile bike ride, visualizing, meditating, eating healthy, throwing my *I Ching* or going to a therapist, I reach out for help. Even if I hate the pain involved, which I do, especially exercise and therapy.

This is apparently a trait of people who succeed. Psychologist Dr. Robert Maurer, in his studies of successful people, has identified four traits of such people, and one of these is that they reach out for help. They reach into the resources around them and get what they need. *They learn what they need to learn. It's all there. But it won't come across the street to you. You have to go and get it.*

At work, I knew how to find mentors, how to learn from them, and move ahead. But I didn't have any guides or mentors for looking inside my own head. Once I found Dr. Levine I saw him three times a week, and began the most painful kind of learning I had done in my life. What I learned from him started me on the climb out of the black hole.

From the therapist I later found in Los Angeles, Dr. Dee Barlow, who has made a special study of women, I learned that I was not alone—that most of the high-powered, high-achieving women in her practice are emotionally very needy, very insecure.

I started at thirty. But it wasn't too late. It's never too late.

You have to deal with Daddy before you marry the wrong man. In my case, before you marry the wrong man again. Without Dr. Levine I could not have understood what happened between my father and me. I would not have understood why I chose the wrong men—a habit it took me years to get over even after I understood it. I would not have been free to go to California.

I was getting vaguely restless. I remembered Joel's prediction: "You'll go to Hollywood." Rocky had reinforced that. No matter how successful the Gucci prank might turn out to be, I did not think my destiny lay in toilet paper.

Dr. Levine demonstrated to me that I had to deal with Daddy first. It took almost three years. So while I was going through this slow, agonizing process, life went on. I had to get the toilet paper to market.

The samples were already made up when Ronnie and I separated. I was still working out of my two-room apartment. The stuff was rolling off the printing press in Rochester by the mile. The packaging looked terrific. You had to get a magnifying glass to see that the *G*'s were really *C*'s. While boxes of samples were arriving at my apartment, the national sales rep who had made the Pet Rock a success was selling it up and down the eastern seaboard.

I helped with the selling in New York. I usually showed it to the big stores myself. At first I was very anxious. Would the buyers get the joke? Yes. Right off. They thought it was hilarious. They started placing big orders, at $3.50 a pair of rolls. I would come home and type invoices at night and, literally, box this stuff and ship it out myself. I could sense a hit. But I really knew I'd made it when Bloomingdale's buyer placed an order. My toilet paper was in Bloomies! Then

Marshall Fields in Chicago, then Filene's in Boston bought in. And Christmas was coming.

It became a sensation. Many magazines and newspapers picked it up. Somebody gave Frank Sinatra eight dozen rolls for Christmas. It was a smash in Florida. A luggage store in Palm Beach called Silvers bought it and put it in their Christmas window. People would come in and buy not two rolls, but forty-eight-roll cases.

Silvers happened to be close to Gucci's store in Palm Beach. People started going into Gucci to ask for the toilet paper instead of going to Silvers. I would have gotten a kick out of it if I'd heard this, but what I didn't know was that Dr. Aldo Gucci was spending Christmas in Palm Beach and could not help but become aware of our little parody. He was not amused.

But, for the moment, I was riding too high to care what criticisms anybody had. The Christmas season was finally over and our toilet paper had been the marketing phenomenon of the year. It was written up in the January 10, 1977, issue of *Time.* In the "Modern Living" section *Time* ran a three-inch story headlined "Rip-Off." Witty, eh? I was thrilled.

"The latest product to sport a chichi monogram is a line of toilet paper imprinted with the initials GC," said *Time.* "The logo closely resembles Gucci's famed trademark, GG. But the initials signify nothing, insists Dawn Steele [sic], whose Manhattan-based Entrepreneuse Enterprises is marketing the rolls for $3.50 a pair. Whatever G.C. really stands for (gross cuteness?), E.E.'s rip-off is a sellout in the New York City area . . ." Etc., etc.

Any story with the headline "Rip-Off" should have sent up a red flag to me that Dr. Gucci and his lawyers would see this and get agitated. But, even though they spelled my name wrong, I was ecstatic. In this issue of *Time*, I was in the company of women who were working on what I saw as important and erudite projects: Shere Hite's *The Hite Report* and Gail Sheehy's *Passages* were on the best-seller list. And I was there with toilet paper.

Next thing I knew, Gucci's lawyers descended, screaming "Infringement of trademark" and "Close her up!" Gucci slapped a restraining order on me, prohibiting me from selling any more toilet paper. I would, of course, fight to get the order lifted. But, in the meantime, they had put me out of business. I wanted to be famous, but this was ridiculous. There it was, a headline on the front page of the *New York Post:* "THE GUCCI TOILET PAPER CAPER."

There'd been so many rip-offs of Gucci. Why pick on us?

A number of years, a hefty amount of litigation and lawyers' fees, and a good deal of anguish later, Ronnie found out why Dr. Gucci was so mad at us even though he didn't go after any of the other rip-offs. What incensed him was that it was toilet paper. He didn't mind dignified rip-offs.

About a week after the *New York Post* headline, the same hawk-eyed court reporter who wrote the first story noticed that I was also being sued for divorce by Ronnie. Actually, it was a civil suit related to our business but, not by coincidence, it occurred as our divorce ground on into an ugly stage. Ronnie wanted a share of the business and I can say now he was entitled to it, but it wasn't really about money. It never is. I believe he was just trying to get my attention.

Soon afterward another headline appeared in the *New York Post*. It read: "THE TRIALS OF DAWN STEEL." That was a nightmare for me. It had been one thing to have my unorthodox business ventures publicized, but my marital problems were another matter. I felt embarrassed and ashamed. My privacy was gone.

"I now know how Warren Beatty feels," I agonized to my mother. (Even in my sorrow, I could be grandiose.)

But my mother loved the headlines. She said, "I think it's great. Now everybody knows you're single, maybe you'll start to date again."

One night, in L.A., a friend took me to a poker game. In the middle of the game, in walked a young, very handsome guy in jeans and motorcycle boots with a pack of cigarettes stuck up the sleeve of his T-shirt. He had just come from a screening of *Harlan County, U.S.A.*, a documentary movie about coal miners, and I thought he was a coal miner. Why would you want to see a coal miner documentary unless you were a coal miner?

We were introduced. Richard what? Richard Gere. None of Richard's movies had opened yet, so I'd never heard of him. He was still an unknown actor, based in New York. He was very, very charming. But I wasn't into him that evening, because I happened to have been distracted by another romance. I noticed Richard in a friendly way (who wouldn't?), but I was too busy brooding about the problems I had with my boyfriend at the time to be attracted.

But we were bonded by the fact that we were the only ones who didn't know how to play poker. It was fun to learn. He sat down beside me and, all evening, Richard and I played the most bungling poker together. I'd show him my hand and ask him, "What have I got here?"

"I don't know. What have I got here?" he'd ask me. Fade out.

Back in New York, I told Margie this story. Margie was still a booking agent for commercials at William Morris. I asked her, "Did you ever hear of a guy called Richard Gere?"

"No," she said.

"I'm telling you," I said, "he's going to be a star."

Margie grabbed her *New York Players Guide,* a huge book that has a mug shot of every actor who's registered with the Screen Actors Guild in New York, and she looked up Richard Gere's picture. She was clearly not impressed.

"He's cute, but I never heard of him. What's he done?"

"Well, his movies aren't out yet," I explained. "But watch this guy, Margie."

She then said to me—and she and I still laugh over it—"You stick to toilet paper and leave talent to me."

But Margie remembered our conversation. A few months later, at a party, Margie was introduced to a young actor. Guess who? He looked as if he needed a shower, his hair was rumpled as if he'd just woken up, he had on a black T-shirt, black jeans and combat boots. Margie couldn't take her eyes off him. Richard really did have that something. Star Quality. She finally saw what I'd been talking about.

I wasn't dating anyone at the time. When Richard wandered away from his date later in the evening, Margie nabbed him in a corner and casually said, "I hear you're the second worst poker player in L.A."

"Where's Dawn?" asked Richard.

That's what friends are for.

He called me, and so began a very magical relationship, an intense, private, very torrid affair with another wrong man. Richard was a man who could never be pinned down (at least not then, and not by me), so he was safe. Again I had picked a man who would, of course, leave me—if I didn't leave him first. This was a situation I was completely comfortable in.

Our affair was very playful, very passionate. He called me Lady Mousse, after my addiction to chocolate mousse.

What I thought of as his outlaw status made him absolutely irresistible to me. He did things differently, outside the system. I saw him as an iconoclast: he lived in a storefront in the East Village. To a lower-middle-class Jewish girl from Great Neck, that's an iconoclast.

He was up for adventure. One night we went to Plato's Retreat, a nude swingers' club in Manhattan where my brother Larry worked as a lifeguard. Larry was still trying to find himself. It was really hard on my mother. Now when her friends would ask "What do your children do?" what was she supposed to say? "My son is a lifeguard at Plato's Retreat and my daughter is in the toilet paper business?"

Actually, Larry did have other interests. If I recall

correctly, his principal activity at the time, aside from his job as a Plato's Retreat lifeguard, was to be the only white guy on a unicycle basketball touring company called UNI-BALL®. (Still nothing there for a mother to work with. . . .)

I'd been hearing about Plato's from Larry, but I'd been too embarrassed to go. Gere, of course, was happy to go. Eventually, we both went in. Neither of us took our clothes off.

What a scene. One of my favorite memories from that night is Larry, in his bathing suit, trying to save this very drunk, overweight older guy who had fallen into the pool. Larry, who didn't want to get into the pool because it was pretty yucky, leaned over to grab this guy by the head and his hand came up with the guy's toupee.

It was a Fellini movie. There were orgy rooms all around the pool. Despite my old *Penthouse* days, this really was not my idea of a good time. I wasn't comfortable. The only place I could get my eyes off the ground was in the merchandising section, where they were selling Plato's Retreat T-shirts and games and gimmicks. That's where I spent most of the evening.

Richard and I did have a lot of fun, but I was never secure in our relationship. I knew there were other women, that he still saw an old girlfriend off and on. I hated it. But I wanted him.

Against the backdrop of romance, I was back in business. The fight with Gucci was still grinding on, but I had started a new business. Ronnie and I were still working together as partners. After he sued me, we didn't speak for four or five months. Our lawyers did all the talking. But one day we had a cup of coffee, pushed the lawyers and the legal problems aside, and resolved everything between ourselves.

Since the restraining order was still in force, we couldn't sell more Gucci toilet paper. Even if we could, we probably wouldn't have. We knew it had been a fad. About six months after the restraining order, in the summer of '77, we started a new company.

We thought up a great name. People would say to me, "What do you do for a living?"

I'd say, "I'm in the toilet paper business."

They would invariably groan, "Oh, Dawn!"

So we called the company Oh Dawn Inc.

This time, we were prepared to pay royalties. I didn't want to go through again what I was going through with Gucci. But it turned out there were plenty of toilet paper ideas that could be packaged with care, gift-wrapped and purveyed to the upscale market. Toilet paper with taste!

We started with "Bloomies." When Bloomingdale's featured us in their Christmas catalog we felt we had enough respectability to move on. We then approached Bantam Books about reprinting the *Book of Lists* that Irving Wallace and his kids had written. We were nervous for months about going there because we were sure a big author like Wallace would consider it a defamation. They loved it. I had been so intimidated by Irwin Shaw. Now Irving Wallace was giving us permission to print his book on toilet paper. It was probably the most successful novelty item that Christmas. Oh Dawn was on a roll.

We did the *James Beard Cookbook* on kitchen

towels, *The People's Almanac,* Doubleday's *Expert Crossword Puzzles* and *The Dieter's Guide to Weight Loss During Sex* on toilet paper—all very successful. We did Superman and The Incredible Hulk on tissues. All with permission, paid up-front royalties, guarantees, negotiated licensing agreements for the exclusive rights for toilet paper, paper towels or tissues. Geniuses.

We branched out into the novelty soap business. Our first item was fortune cookies made out of soap packaged in Chinese take-out food containers. For the fortunes, we brainstormed with our friends and searched Confucius for sayings. The fortune cookies were a big hit, and we went on to do more soaps. Twinkies in soap, Hostess chocolate cupcakes, Life Savers, Popsicles. I was on the road a lot of the time, selling. Business was great.

Around this time Gucci finally agreed on a settlement. They didn't ask for any of the profits back, but the restraining order stood. I agreed to stop printing and selling the Designer Toilet Paper. The plates were burned. The Great Gucci Toilet Paper Caper was over.

Meanwhile, the affair with Gere was also over. Our romance had run its course. I'd hoped he was the right man, but I knew he wasn't. I could never have him the way that I wanted to have a man—equal, trusting, there. I knew, on some unconscious level, that he could devastate me. That if I stayed with him I would get hurt because he was the kind of guy I could be completely obsessed with. Wonderfully charming, handsome, sexual, interesting, but, like my other men, cut off. My instincts—this inner voice—made me always stop short, just short, of disaster. I had to leave him before he could leave me. And I did.

I had a perfect way to end it. Richard was moving to London to shoot a movie called *Yanks*. I helped him pack his stuff and move out of his East Village storefront. He had a bed, thousands of paperback books, a couple of pairs of jeans. We packed everything in boxes. We stuffed the boxes on a friend's truck and put them in storage.

He came to my place for our last night together. We gave each other gifts. He gave me a Victorian clock we called Lady Mousse. I gave him luggage.

I knew Richard was not the love of my life but it was hard to let him go. And he kept teasing me with calls and postcards. In May of 1978, there came a card from Manchester: "Could use your company right now . . . Earth to Richard, Earth to Richard. Richard to Dawn, Richard to Dawn. Come in. Come in . . ."

Damn him. His birthday was coming up at the end of August, so I telegrammed him and told him there was a birthday surprise coming. I flew to London and called him from the airport. A girl answered. Then Richard came on, stuttering something or other.

He came to my hotel to talk about it but what could he say or do? My fantasies were over.

I could sit in a hotel in London in the rain and feel sorry for myself. Or I could pick myself up. I called the concierge and asked, "What is the first plane out of here?" He booked me on a flight to Rome the following morning.

For two weeks, I roamed Venice, Florence, Capri, Milan, Positano, Monaco. I met people. I met men who said I was beautiful. I met women who, like me, had decided to see the world. I made friends. People talk to you when you're traveling alone. I went on my instincts in terms of who to talk to and I never felt that anyone would hurt me. I was shy about talking to people sometimes, but as soon as I smiled they smiled back.

I began to heal. By the time I got to Milan, my shopping instinct had revived. Even though I did maintain a very romantic, tragic and melancholy aura around my trip, I forced myself to keep moving on. It worked. The journey wound up becoming a magic, transforming trip as well as an education.

This is a very important lesson: *Don't feel sorry for yourself. Get up off the floor. Keep moving. And maintain your dignity at all costs—in love as well as in business.* You may be hurt. You may cry. But it isn't the end of the world. You haven't lost the most important person in the world: yourself.

Finally, I felt ready to come home and get on with my life. On my way back, I called Richard from Monte Carlo and he was frantic. "Where have you been? I've been worried sick. Are you coming back? I want to see you."

"You have no right to be worried about me," I said.

But, of course, I went to see him when I went back through London. He took me to dinner but we didn't sleep together. It was over.

When I came home, two of his movies were breaking. *Blood Brothers* had just opened. *Days of Heaven* was coming as well. His face was on the cover of so many magazines. I couldn't get away from his image and it was difficult for me. But I had held on to my dignity. Barely.

I was beginning to understand my obsession with the wrong men. I had continued, doggedly, to see Dr. Levine three times each week. It was horrendously painful.

I remember walking down Fifth Avenue with Margie, desperate because Dr. Levine was questioning me about my dreams. What dreams? "Margie, how do you remember your dreams? I can't remember any. I have no dreams." But he was helping me see, for the first time, that my anger with my father wasn't about money or about how miserable the lack of it had made me. It was about my father's being closed to me. Before I could get myself to stop going after these men who couldn't be pinned down, I would have to come to grips with my father's inability to nurture me as a child, and I would have to understand, too, the positive things he had given me. And I had to forgive him.

We had to peel away layers of anger and resentment. I'd perceived my father as an economic failure. But Dr. Levine showed me that my father, despite a devastating illness, had not totally abandoned my mother and us, but had struggled back to work and helped to keep a roof over our head and food on the table. Dr. Levine showed me that my father had a great instinct for survival, and deserved my respect. I began to understand that even though my father was imperfect, he had vanquished awesome demons to survive emotionally.

My father became a hero to me again. And I began to feel I could be released from him. I forgave him. I was growing up.

I'd taken a big step toward forgiving myself when I forgave my father. It turned out that if I stopped blaming him I could also stop blaming myself. Just as I could never give him any credit, I could never give myself credit for anything either.

Dr. Levine woke me up. He helped me see that I had to separate from my parents. I had to separate from their darkness. I needed to take some risks and get unstuck.

It was time for a change. It seemed to me that, to begin with, it was time to branch out in a new direction in my work life. After some deliberation, I finally decided that what I wanted to do was to open a gift store in Greenwich Village. Really.

One day, Margie and I went downtown to scout for a location. We looked at a neat place on West Fourth street and I told the landlords I would think about it. They were never to hear from me.

That night, I was on the phone with my friend, Craig Baumgarten, then a junior production executive at Paramount, and he said to me, "You know, if you can merchandise smut at *Penthouse* and you can merchandise toilet paper, then you can merchandise the movie business." Sounded logical to me. "Come to L.A.," he said, "and I'll introduce you to people." Oh, okay.

I left for Los Angeles the very next week. I had a

little money and a couple of friends. I was still carrying a load of fear and anger along with my hopes. But, thanks to Dr. Levine, I could at least look up and see a way out of the black hole I had climbed into as a kid. In California, I started to step out into the light.

BOOK TWO

THE BREAK OF DAWN

7

STAR TREK:
THE ASHTRAY

1978. Jimmy Carter is president. Punk rocker Sid vicious is arrested for killing his girlfriend. *Grease, Superman* and *National Lampoon's Animal House* break box office records. The Bee Gees wipe the charts clean with "Night Fever" and "Stayin' Alive," making it clear that *Saturday Night Fever* will have an extraordinarily long-lasting presence and influence on pop culture.

My first night in Hollywood was a combination of Greek tragedy and screwball comedy. My friend Nat Lehrman, then the publisher of *Playboy* magazine, was in town and he offered to take me to the Playboy Mansion.

"L.A. is not L.A.," Nat informed me, "without a visit to the Mansion." Nat was incredibly well-read, erudite and witty. He was like Oscar Wilde to me. Oscar Wilde, that is, if he'd had a friend named Hugh Hefner.

I had checked into a hotel and he came to get me. On the way we picked up his friend Nancy Collins, who was a reporter for *Women's Wear Daily* at the time. She was blond, beautiful, brilliant and impossibly tall, and completely confident. I liked her anyway.

We drove through the heart of Beverly Hills, through more wealth than I had ever seen. We turned into a long driveway, rolled by sweeping landscaped grounds and arrived at the fantastic mansion of legend. At the door, Nat turned to me and he said: "Please remember: Don't take anything personally."

Nancy got more attention than I did. She was not only a Grace Kelly look-alike, with legs that were longer than my entire body, she also had great arms. I remember this one poor guy had the bad idea to hit on her. She looked down on him—she looked down on everybody—and she said, very slowly, "Beat it, buster." There was a woman who didn't have to worry about finding a voice. She'd never lost hers.

We wandered around viewing the clusters of semi-nude girls and randy guys. Boobs. More boobs. This was boob city. Inside, people were dancing, drinking, flirting. It felt like a brothel for foreplay.

The Greek tragedy part was that the place was full of actors who were just about all has-beens. It was like a warning about what happens to you when your phone stops ringing. If someone had tried to invent a Hollywood purgatory for me, they couldn't have done better than this lavish place full of playmates with huge breasts and has-been actors and no one paying attention to me. For this, I'd left New York?

I will never survive this, I thought.

In some way, my first night out at the Playboy Mansion pretty much characterized my early experiences in Los Angeles: I couldn't figure out how the hell I was going to survive what was happening to me. At the Mansion, it had been pretty specific and concentrated. I felt: I'm shorter than everyone, I have smaller breasts, I'm not as glamorous-looking as these bunnies.

But in L.A. at large, and in the movie business, I sort of felt the same way. People I met weren't just pretty, blond and healthy-looking. Some of them were also very smart and very well connected.

I felt like a Martian. I was thirty-two years old. I had had three prior careers. And now I was starting from scratch.

Only, I couldn't find a job. I spent months interviewing. Craig introduced me to people and my only other friend, Bob Finkelstein, introduced me to people, but I just didn't have enough contacts.

And I was always getting lost. I had and still have the worst sense of direction in the history of driving. It took me forever to feel comfortable driving in Los Angeles because there were no numbers on the streets. I had a little bit of money from having sold my company to Ronnie, so I rented a Fiat, a little red convertible. Stick shift, of course. I had never driven stick, and on the streets with hills, I could not learn to downshift. I went up a hill, my car would stall and I'd be sitting there thinking I'm never going to figure this out, ever. It took me a long time to feel like I was on terra firma.

I didn't know it then, but the movie business was also in a state of transition. Not only was the old guard out but also the first wave of reaction, the Baby Moguls phenomenon, was just peaking. All these brilliant kids had shipped out of New York in their VW Beetles and BMWs, with their jeans and beards, and come to Hollywood to save the world. Veteran radical activists all of twenty-three or twenty-four, they came to make movies of significance. Francis Coppola was a guru. Mythic epics like *Star Wars* were one type of model, but political content became more and more de rigueur. *The Deer Hunter* was just coming out. But it was *Apocalypse Now* that everyone was waiting for.

I wasn't like the Baby Moguls. They had all graduated from college. They were all literate. They were all committed political activists. I was none of those things.

But a second wave had already started to roll, and that was created by people who were much more like me. It was a whole different atmosphere.

It was about capturing the spirit of the times with high-concept pictures geared to the youth audience— movies whose themes could be explained in a sentence or two. These were movies like *Saturday Night Fever* that were, as they were called at the time, critic-proof, so that they could bypass all the old ways of thinking. Drawn to their theme, audiences would come to see them whatever their reviews were.

Paramount was the hub of the new high-concept think, and I was thrilled when Richard Weston, whom Craig had introduced me to, called me to come and interview at Paramount. At the time Richard Weston was vice-president of merchandising. But he wanted to be head of television, though I didn't know it then. So he was looking to hire someone who he felt could take his job, which was a really rare opportunity. I was desperate for this job, which paid $37,000 a year. But first I had to meet Dick Zimbert, a senior vice-president, an éminence grise. And if I made it through that trial, then I would have to meet Michael Eisner, the president of the studio.

Thank God that Dick Zimbert loved me. In fact, as it turned out, he became a mentor to me and stayed my friend the whole time I was at Paramount. After our initial interview, he told Michael Eisner he had to meet me, and I prepared myself for that encounter with a great deal of anticipation. To this day I don't know why Michael was meeting people at that level but maybe he knew Richard Weston was going to be leaving.

You have to understand how intimidating a guy like Michael Eisner would have been to me. Michael was and is one of the smartest people in the entertainment industry. He was a power in programming at ABC Television, and Paramount's chairman, Barry Diller, his old boss at ABC, had brought him into Paramount to run both movies and television. Michael Eisner was unusually well educated for someone in the high-concept crowd. He's a very likable, very tall, very cute, very sly person. He's got this seemingly easy-going, open appearance, so some people say he seems whimsical. He is. But he's an extremely complex man, at once brilliant and childlike.

The meeting terrified me because I wanted the job so badly and, in the past, I tended to close up when I wanted something that badly. But the meeting was great. Michael was the most ebullient man I'd ever met. He just drew me out and I responded to his interest. He was very relaxed, asking questions like

"Who are you? Where do you come from?" And, somehow, I just got into it and started telling him the story of my life.

It was not only a great job interview but I got a major lesson in corporate management: *You need to know how to make people comfortable so that they'll give you their best ideas, their best energy.*

This was the thing about Michael. During the interview, he made me feel that I was the only person who existed on earth at that moment. He was so interested that I told it all—the sports job, *Penthouse,* Gucci toilet paper, the lawsuits, the headlines, the works.

When I concluded my saga, Michael laughed and declared: "It's a television series, like *Rhoda.* This'll be *The Dawn Steel Story,* starring Penny Marshall."

Eisner got a lifelong fan. I got a job.

I turned off Melrose Avenue into the Paramount Studios complex for my first day of work wondering what the hell I was supposed to do. Of course, as I pulled up in my rented Fiat (I counted myself lucky if I didn't stall before I managed to park), I thought of some of the greats who had come before me. Cecil B. De Mille and Adolph Zukor had worked at Paramount. And here I was. The old days were gone, but high-concept musicals like *Saturday Night Fever* and *Grease* and *Urban Cowboy* were coming out of Paramount when I arrived.

When I'd come for my two previous interviews, my friend Craig had shepherded me from the parking lot to Richard Weston's and Michael Eisner's offices. Now I was alone. I managed to park the Fiat but then, of course, immediately lost my sense of direction. Lost in the parking lot. Great.

There was no one around. Not a soul. Feeling very uncertain and disoriented, I just wandered around for a while, trying to figure out where to go. Then I saw an information booth.

I'd now been roaming around for twenty minutes, so I remember thinking how good that information booth looked. I gratefully marched up to the window only to find that it was a facade—a set. And then as I stood there, uncertain whether I should find this hilarious or catastrophic, I picked my head up, and walking toward me from the left was John Travolta and walking toward me from the right was Warren Beatty. I remember thinking, I'm either on Mars or in heaven.

So where were the cameras?

Nowhere near my cubbyhole of an office, I'll tell you that. I started as director of merchandising and for a long time I didn't see a camera or anything else that had to do with actual moviemaking. My job was to help market movies and television series by developing products and promoting them. Instead of marketing Penis Plants, I was supposed to market *Mork and Mindy* suspenders (Mork, as you may remember, was Robin Williams's first big job), as well as products for other Paramount shows like *Happy Days* and *Laverne and Shirley* or movies such as *Urban Cowboy*.

I remember sitting there the first day, thinking, "I have nothing to do. What am I supposed to do? Who am I supposed to call?"

So they told me to start reading files. Richard Weston sent over a huge bunch of documents for me to read and I plowed through an enormous number of contracts to learn what made a good licensing deal. In the beginning it was slow going, but gradually Richard brought me into all meetings with him and would turn over whatever happened in that meeting to me.

Richard was a very smart man. In one meeting, he asked me a question about the status of one of our projects. I didn't know the answer. But rather than say, "I don't know, I'll look into it," I panicked. And I spoke from the hip.

Richard looked at me and said, "You're winging it, aren't you?"

He was right. I was. I never did that again. *If you don't know something, it is better to say, "I don't know, I'll find out," than it is to pretend you do. There is no shame in not knowing.*

By then Richard had made it clear he was leaving and I learned everything I could learn from him. I was really lucky. Not only was Richard Weston a very skilled teacher but also he was unthreatened by me (or anyone else). On the contrary, he got a lot of satisfaction from helping me.

It was a very easy job for me. I picked it up like a natural, because I understood it. I understood how merchandising could be integrated into the company's marketing and I also saw how I could turn merchandising, which had not been an important profit center before, into a profit center that would help reduce marketing costs.

The work was going well, but I felt isolated. My little cubicle of an office was in a building across the way from the main administration building where my senior colleagues sat. There wasn't even a place for a secretary yet. I sat there by myself. I was lonely.

In those early days, I was slowly starting to meet other people at Paramount. I began to have some contact with a few of the marketing people when I discovered that what I did in merchandising should be connected to what they did in the marketing department. Organizationally, merchandising had never been part of marketing. It seemed only logical to me that it should be.

Lucky for me, Frank Mancuso encouraged me. Frank was head of marketing and distribution. Paternal, and familial, he made me feel part of the marketing family.

My operation was basically a small stand-alone division that nobody really paid any attention to up until that time. I tried to make my little area as much a part of the marketing division as I could. There's a lesson there: *If you're in a small pond, find a bigger connection. Hook up to a large pond, one way or another.*

I was starting to integrate myself into the Hollywood community. I spent a huge amount of time just working. I wasn't going out with anyone, but at night I'd go to parties or to the industry screenings. We hung around in packs. We were singles, and obsessed with our work. It was like one gigantic network.

Little by little, I got more professional exposure in the company, too. I think the turning point came at an event called a divisional meeting. This particular meeting was held at La Costa, a resort near San Diego.

Every vice-president and up in every division throughout the company, throughout the world, came to these meetings. Each Paramount executive gave a presentation. You were expected to describe what you were doing, what you expected to be doing in the future, and somehow demonstrate how you could work within the company synergistically.

My friend Larry Mark, who had just been promoted to vice-president of production from vice-president of West Coast marketing, and I drove down together. We were panicked; not only were we attending our first divisional, but also on the agenda was the dreaded and legendary "new ideas" meeting in which we had to come up with an idea for a movie and pitch it to the whole group.

Larry hated the idea of pitching in public even worse than I did. In the first hour we drove to San Diego, we tried to figure out ways to get out of it; we thought of doctors' notes, coming down with the flu, or perhaps getting a flat tire so we would miss the new ideas meeting altogether. In the next hour of driving, resigned, we rehearsed and criticized our pitches over and over. I played Michael Eisner, Larry played himself. Larry played Michael Eisner and I played myself.

By the time we arrived, we both thought we were Michael Eisner. And we were just as panicked as when we started.

I don't remember Larry's, but my presentation was called "Eve's Rib," a title Larry thought up in the car. It was a reverse Pygmalion about a young woman executive in an automotive company who kept trying to get promoted. She couldn't get past VP, even though she did great work and she did everything she was supposed to do. Men around her, below her, got promoted, but not our heroine. She couldn't figure it out.

So finally she made a bet with a friend of hers. She saw a guy walking by in the mailroom and she said to her friend, "I bet you I can turn that guy into an executive who gets promoted faster than I do." So she took this guy from the mailroom and she groomed him. She taught him how to talk and taught him how the business worked and taught him how to make presentations and he rose very quickly through the ranks of this corporation.

Then they fell in love.

There were two best new ideas at the meeting. Mine was one. The other one was about a female Indian chief. Neither ever got made. But that was irrelevant. What was important was that Senior Vice-President of Production Don Simpson was there, and he liked my idea.

Six months after I started at Paramount, Richard Weston moved into television. I was promoted to vice-president of merchandising and licensing for Paramount's television and feature properties. And then I found myself in the middle of a nightmare called *Star Trek: The Motion Picture*.

The movie was in production. It was in deep trouble. Talk about overbudgeted movies. . . . It would eventually cost $44 million, an amazing amount for a movie in 1979. An amazing amount today. It was hard to figure out how, but Special Effects, always the black hole of filmmaking, had wasted an enormous amount of money. And not one effect was ready.

My job couldn't have been tougher. I wanted to convince manufacturers to feature the *Star Trek* logos, themes and characters on their products. But there was no film to show them. In order to get a toy company or a pajama company to manufacture and merchandise products using our logo, or to get Coca-Cola to do a promotional tie-in, using Star Trek characters in their ads, I had to show these companies some footage and tell them when the movie was going to be released. Well, we had no idea when it was going to be finished and there was no footage ready. Brilliantly, the debacle had been kept under wraps, but we were headed for a budget disaster on the scale of *Heaven's Gate*'s.

Emergency measures were called for. For starters, Jeffrey Katzenberg was brought out from New York. He had been Diller's assistant and even then, at the age of twenty-eight or twenty-nine, Jeffrey had a reputation as a "can-do" kind of guy. He moved his office and his desk to the special effects laboratory, overseeing the entire process. He was the one who was responsible for getting this movie finished, which never would have been done without him.

I had a connection to Jeffrey. He was the best friend of Sid Davidoff, my lawyer in the Gucci affair. What we didn't have in common is that he was raised, as Eisner was, on Park Avenue. His father was a stockbroker. He went to private schools. But he was an NYU dropout like me. He was a gambler like me. In fact, my gambling career with Neil was small potatoes compared to Jeffrey's. He had been virtually run out of the Bahamas for card-counting in blackjack.

Davidoff had described him to me as "four feet ten inches, ninety pounds soaking wet, a pit bull, tenacious as hell." That was Jeffrey. But he was taller.

My first sighting of him was on the stairs outside the producer Frank Yablans's office. I saw him run up the stairs, run into Yablans's office and then run out of Yablans's office down the stairs. I thought, This guy's like Roadrunner. Beep. Beep.

Jeffrey Katzenberg at this time was a VP and assistant to Paramount's production chief, Don Simpson. Simpson was one of the Baby Moguls, an excessive bear of a man, bearded, with one of the most colorful vocabularies of anyone I've ever known. And, of course, I was wildly attracted to him. He had an undisciplined but dazzling mind and could accomplish wonders in a business where leaps of the imagination were often more effective than any other strategy.

An Officer and a Gentleman was a good example of a Don Simpson miracle. It was one of his notorious saves—a disaster that he turned into gold. Gere, who only wanted to do art films, didn't want to do it. It was too commercial for him and he had to be dragged, kicking and screaming, into it. He and Debra Winger were at each other like cats and dogs. The script needed work. Simpson wrangled one of the hottest directors at the moment, Taylor Hackford, made peace among the warring parties, bulldozed the script through, kept his vision of the story despite everyone else's distraction, and wound up saving the movie and turning it into a big hit.

Don Simpson and Jeffrey together were in charge of turning *Star Trek* into a movie. The story goes that Simpson tried to talk Jeffrey out of it, that he said to him: *"Star Trek* is a nighttime freight train. It's bearing down on you at two hundred miles per hour. Get off the fucking track!" He didn't. It wasn't in Jeffrey's nature to get off the track.

My job was to merchandise this runaway freight train. I was deeply concerned about my ability to pull it off. It was a great opportunity. But there was no movie and no precedent for what I was doing—promotional tie-ins and merchandising on this huge scale.

This was not Penis Plants. This was *STAR TREK!* It had a cult following and mythic status around the world. There had to be an audience waiting for plastic toy *Starship Enterprises* and Mr. Spock ears.

But despite *Star Trek's* cult following, there still remained a substantial portion of the American population who were not Trekkies. What did they know of Spock ears? My job was to sell a movie that didn't exist yet to an audience that didn't exist yet.

But how?

I would put on a show, a spectacular production. I would invite all the toy and merchandise tie-in manufacturers to an event they would never forget. So we had no film to show, no special effects. But we had the stars; Captain Kirk, Mr. Spock, Bones, Scotty and the rest of the crew of the *Starship Enterprise.*

There was a woman who was doing promotion at Paramount at the time whose name was Brenda Mutchnick. She was great at her job, which was to market educational films. She helped me put together a presentation. We wrote a script, hired a director and prepared a budget.

But first I had to sell the idea at another company-wide divisional meeting. Every department head in the company, the entire production division, every senior executive at Paramount, all of them were sitting around a horseshoe-shaped table. The only other female executive was Maggie Wilde, who was one of my first friends in the movie business. All of the other women there were taking notes. I had to give the *Star Trek* merchandising presentation in front of Paramount studio president Michael Eisner. In front of Charlie Bluhdorn, Gulf & Western's chairman. In front of Paramount chairman Barry Diller. In front of distribution and marketing president Frank Mancuso.

My report was ready, but my voice was gone. It was like being back in the sixth grade. When Barry Diller walked into the room, I was rendered speechless. He was intimidating, he knew it and he enjoyed it. He just kind of gazed at me with this chilling look.

I had to find a way to bring these guys down to my level. As I faced Diller and Eisner, I knew this was the time for some creative visualization. I had to come up with images of these men that would knock them off Mount Olympus.

And I did. I won't tell you how I pictured all of them in my mind. But trust me when I tell you, it was the great equalizer.

I was able to stand up and give my report. I'm sure I stuttered, but I spoke. I got through it, and some people clapped. They applauded! It felt great. I filed some of that good feeling away so that I could call on it next time I needed it. And I would need it. A lot.

My report was given the green light. Now the show could go on.

We held it in the largest theater on the Paramount lot to accommodate all the prospective manufacturers of licensed merchandise like T-shirts, hats and pajamas; the big chain store buyers from Kmart, JCPenney and Sears, who would buy the *Star Trek* merchandise; and executives from my hoped-for promotional partners, McDonald's and Coca-Cola.

The show began. I held my breath as I was beamed onto the stage with lasers. There were gasps and appreciative applause from the audience. Let's say that it was definitely not your average marketing presentation. . . .

I snapped into a running dialogue with a Hal-like computer. Then this dazzling multimedia presentation unfolded. Every minute, the lasers went *tut-a-tttut,* and, zap, there was Leonard Nimoy. Zap, William Shatner. Then James Doohan, who played Scotty. As the entire *Star Trek* cast was beamed up on the stage the audience just went crazy. Remember, these actors had been off the screen for years. Then I took the mike and went into the audience like Oprah, to do stand-up with *Star Trek* trivia questions.

The next day in the coffee shop that was a kind of commissary, Michael Eisner yelled across the room, "Dawn, I want to see you in my office tomorrow at eleven." Unbeknownst to me, he had been in the audience with Don Simpson. I was sure he must have hated it and that he was going to fire me.

I went into his office the next morning and blurted out, "Michael, was it something I said?"

He ignored me. "Okay, what do you want to do with your life?" he asked me.

He wasn't going to fire me. But what was I supposed to tell him? I liked television. TV looked like fun.

"Well, Michael, television could be very . . ." I started to say.

"Forget what you want to do. This is what I've done. Get *Star Trek* finished up. Then you're vice-president of production in Features. Congratulations."

"I don't know anything about movies," I told him.

"Neither does anybody else. Good-bye, good luck and break a leg!"

What a fantastic break that was.

Don Simpson, now president of production, phoned me from London. "It was my idea," he said. I thanked him, laughed and hung up.

But suddenly, I was filled with anxiety: "What am I going to do when they find out I don't know what I'm doing."

This is apparently a very common anxiety. A business magazine once did a survey that found that this feeling of fraudulence surfaces as one of the most common fears executives have. But I didn't know that for a long time. I thought it was just me.

But before I could switch to my new production job, I had to convert the *Star Trek* presentation into a merchandising success. I had to get the *Starship Enterprise* and its crew out there on battery-operated toys, Band-Aids, pajamas and anything else I, or anyone else, could think of. I did manage to convince McDonald's and Coca-Cola to do a tie-in. That was no easy job to begin with, and then I had trouble at the other end because I couldn't get Bill Shatner or Leonard Nimoy to do it.

So I went back to McDonald's and Coca-Cola and convinced them to use Klingons instead. The Klingons, I suggested, could be eating Big Macs and drinking Cokes in their commercials. The commercials had to be ready to bombard the nation in December '79, the month *Star Trek* was to be released.

I flew back to New York to show the commercials to Diller at the Gulf & Western headquarters. As far as I could tell, he was impressed. When he saw the Klingons eating Big Macs and drinking Coca-Cola, he laughed—the first time I had ever seen him laugh. I was thrilled.

By then I had been working on the merchandising of *Star Trek* night and day for six months and I felt as if I had pulled off some miracles. Besides the commercials, the *Star Trek* emblem would be on every McDonald's carton and every paper cup with Coke in it. Coca-Cola and McDonald's were paying millions for the tie-in, on top of spending tens of millions to pay for network advertising to promote our film. I heard that word about me was getting around.

After the presentation, I was about to take the elevator down from the thirty-third floor and I was holding the door, talking to Art Barron, my other mentor, the chief financial officer whom I was so fond of. Suddenly I heard this voice with a thick Viennese accent coming from the back of the elevator. "Ms. Steel, would you close the elevator doors?"

I swung around. "Oh, my God, Mr. Bluhdorn! I'm sorry." I closed the elevator doors and Charlie Bluhdorn taught me a lesson I never forgot.

As the elevator went down thirty-three floors, he recited to me every single thing I had done since I joined Paramount. Not only did he know my name, he knew every television show I'd merchandised and every product we'd licensed. He knew the *Star Trek* presentation. He had seen the McDonald's–Coke commercials, and he was able to recite the details of the entire campaign. I was knocked out.

It pumped me up so much that it kept me going for years. Every time I'd be stuck or scared or depressed, I'd think about Charlie Bluhdorn in that elevator. It's sad to think that some people never bump into a Charlie Bluhdorn. Most people don't ever have that elevator ride. I really got lucky there.

On December 7, 1979, Frank Mancuso invited me to a pre-Christmas dinner at his home in New Jersey to celebrate what we hoped would be *Star Trek's* huge opening. It was a very familial evening: Frank, his wife, his children and me.

In mid-evening, we left the house and drove around New Jersey, checking the lines outside all the theaters where *Star Trek* had opened earlier that day. It was thrilling. Lines snaked around blocks, as far as the eye could see. I turned to Frank and said, "So this is what it feels like." He hugged me.

On May 12, 1980, in the "On the Move" column of *Box Office,* there was a postage-stamp picture of me and a tiny, tiny story announcing that "Dawn Steel has been named vice-president of production for Paramount Pictures." They spelled my name right.

What did you actually do in production? I had no idea. But production did not look like a bad place for a woman. Sherry Lansing had just been made president of Twentieth Century–Fox Productions, the first woman to be given that job. Lucy Fisher and Paula Weinstein were coming up the ranks at Zoetrope and at United Artists, respectively. I was excited.

But I really knew I had made it when I was leafing through *The New Yorker* one day, and there was a cartoon that bore the caption: "Star Trek: The Ashtray."

8

LIKE A
SPONGE

1980. RONALD REAGAN IS ELECTED PRESIDENT. JOHN
Lennon is assassinated. Indira Gandhi gains the ma-
jority of votes in India's legislative elections. Iranian
women protest at the president's office in Teheran
over the Islamic dress code. Marjorie Matthews, a
Methodist minister, becomes the first woman bishop
of a U.S. church. The year's hit songs include Bette
Midler's "The Rose," Streisand and Gibb's "Guilty"
and John Lennon's "(Just Like) Starting Over." The
big movies are *The Empire Strikes Back, Nine to Five,
Private Benjamin, Urban Cowboy, Airplane* and *Raging Bull.* The movie industry learns just how big a flop
you can have when *Heaven's Gate* makes headlines as
film history's biggest bust.

* * *

It was my first day in production. I was sitting at my desk, sort of dazed, trying to read a script, which I didn't know how to do. I had never read a script before. Actually, there were quite a few things I didn't know: what the word "turnaround" meant, what a gaffer did, what my job really was.

The door swung open and a tall, handsome man walked in. It was Jeff Berg, who was eventually to become head of I.C.M. Even then, he was a very important and powerful agent.

He said, "Hi, my name is Jeff Berg and I'm with I.C.M. I look forward to doing a lot of business with you."

He had me for life. In the years that followed, we had many dealings, and I'm sure that he got the benefit of the doubt more often than not because of his foresight. *On my very first day as a production executive, he treated me like a person before I was officially declared to be a person. . . .*

That was a good lesson. It was good business and I did the same when new people came in, either at an agency or my studio or any studio.

I had my work cut out for me, wending my way in my new milieu and absorbing the huge amount of new information I would need to even begin to function in my new job. I became a sponge. I knew Michael Eisner and Don Simpson had taken a chance on me, that they were hoping that my instincts for what made a successful widget would be applicable to what makes a successful movie, and I certainly wanted to prove them right. The only problem was I didn't know anything about making movies.

I was in a state of high anxiety all the time, every

second, and I stayed in a state of high anxiety until I left Columbia Pictures, five job titles later. I didn't know it at the time, but this is the natural state of the Hollywood executive. I thought it was just me, caused by what I didn't know, hadn't done, needed to prove. So I pounced on the problem with all the energy and subtlety of a tank.

I arrived, as I did in merchandising, saying "What am I supposed to do? Who am I supposed to call?" I was a junior production executive. What did that mean? My job—or the job of any production executive—was to get a movie made, any way, any how. But what did "Get a movie made" mean?

Don explained. My job was not only to find and develop movie ideas, but also to establish relationships with "talent"—directors, writers, producers, actors—and their agents and lawyers. My job was to convince them to bring their ideas to me. Not to another studio, not to another executive, but to me. Or, as Katzenberg called it, "reeling in the tuna."

Every weekend, junior people like me were expected to read what came in during the week. What was invariably referred to as The Dreaded Weekend Read List consisted of scripts, articles, plays, short stories, song lyrics, foreign movies or old movies that could be remade.

On Monday mornings we would all discuss what we had read. We would all advocate our own ideas.

Now came the problem.

Even if you are a vice president of production, you have no authority. You can't buy material, you can only advocate or influence. Diller ran Paramount on an advocacy basis. At that point, the studio was making maybe fifteen movies a year. It was up to me to try to make at least two of those movies mine. But no one in the room wanted those movies to be mine. Nobody supported any ideas except his or her own. Practically speaking, what this means is that all ideas were shot down by the group.

So I finally figured out that the way to get my ideas past the junior exec barrier was not to pitch the ideas in the group, but to find someone in a position of authority and pitch one on one.

In some corporations, this group-kill of ideas is a very common configuration. There are many ways to figure a way around it. Find one.

I learned my job by doing and watching. I knew I was able to recognize a good idea, which was a key skill. But I had to learn where to find those ideas and how to develop them. Meetings were crucial. Who to have a meeting with, what to say and how to listen.

Because of the constant need for material, the meetings with people outside the company were as important as the internal meetings. My friend Craig Baumgarten took me to every meeting he had with agents, writers and producers who pitched him movie ideas. He also took me to every breakfast, lunch and dinner. It was a crash course on the art and science of the pitch, on learning to gauge what stories might work, what stories could never work, what talent was available, what material was around. Craig was responsible for the beginnings of many of my working relationships.

At the office, I followed Jeffrey Katzenberg around all the time. I sat in on meetings with him. I went to meetings with Don Simpson. I read scripts. People were always on the lookout for interesting scripts for me to read, not even to make into movies, but just to learn about scripts. They'd say, "You should read such and such a script, it's really great," so that I began to get a sense of what great writing was. In between, I sat in people's offices and listened, absorbing information. I didn't talk much in these meetings because I didn't have the confidence to talk and, truthfully, I didn't have much to say.

It's a simple but important lesson: *Listen.*

Now whenever I'm trying to train someone, I always tell them to just sit in my office and listen the way I used to listen to those guys. You can't beat that for an education. And pretty soon, if you sit there long enough, someone's going to come up with something they need you to do.

One day, Jeffrey asked me to take notes, literally, on a reel-by-reel examination he did of a movie called *Going Ape!* That was Jeffrey's way of looking at a rough cut. A rough cut is a kind of rough draft of a movie: movies are made in pieces and a rough cut draws the pieces together. When you shoot a scene, you usually have several camera angles on the same action. In a rough cut, you "roughly" put these together, so that the scene is linear, and then you put these scenes in a sequence. What Jeffrey and I were looking at was in essence the first draft of a movie.

We looked at the whole thing once and then went back and looked at each reel and Jeffrey gave the producer and director his notes. This was a movie that featured Danny DeVito and Tony Danza chasing apes. At that time, Paramount was also releasing *Urban Cowboy,* starring Debra Winger and John Travolta. Here I was finally working on a picture and what star did I get to work with? Danny or Tony? Nah. Debra or John? Nope. I was in charge of the ape.

But never mind. The ape was a great contact. He introduced me to Danny and Tony. In Hollywood, as in many places, relationships are essential to getting anything done. You meet people in strange places and they pop up elsewhere in your life. I met Robin Williams when I was still in merchandising; I needed to get his approval so I could put his face on a T-shirt when he was doing *Mork and Mindy.* He would eventually bring me *Good Morning, Vietnam* and we would make *Awakenings* together. I met Kevin Costner when he was an unemployed actor we hired to work with actresses on screen tests for *Flashdance.*

I met an incredible number of people in my early days in production. Some by chance, others I'd seek out, while others—for the first time since I'd gotten to Los Angeles—would find me.

My very first day in production, I got a call from Joel Silver, a young assistant to successful producer Larry Gordon, whose office was next to my little office. He came from New Jersey and NYU film school. He told me he'd heard "the lore on the lot that says that Dawn Steel had done a very impressive job of helping to promote the first *Star Trek* feature." And he had just called to say, in one long run-on sentence in the fastest English I ever heard, "I-want-to-be-on-your-call-list-every-single-day — I-have-a-great-working-knowledge-of-the-workings-of-the-lot-and-of-the-business-you-can-call-every-day-and-you-can-ask-the-dumbest-questions-you-can-possibly-think-of-you-call-me-every-day-every-single-day." I did. And he answered every single question.

Joel eventually became Larry Gordon's partner and made, among others, two *Die Hard*s and three *Lethal Weapon*s. Joel was a fascinating character. And still is. He was, even then, an encyclopedia of information, not just about movies but about art. He was an expert on Frank Lloyd Wright and modernist architecture. This man, who once said, "I don't make art; I buy it," has great wit and an extraordinary overview of the business. I learned an enormous amount from him.

In that very first conversation, he also said, *"Preface everything you say by saying 'I don't know anything, but here's what I think,' and they won't think you're arrogant."* He was right.

I was learning from everyone, at the office, at parties, everywhere. The person who probably taught me the most about getting noticed was Cher. I met her at a party. She was standing in the kitchen and she had cut off all of her hair and what she had left was white. She was dressed all in black with crucifix earrings. Cher was very punk and looked fantastic. I loved her on sight because she was completely original. Most of all, she dared to be herself.

I could see how wonderfully well Cher's style worked for her, and what a great way it was to attract attention to herself, which is what I wanted to do when I walked into a room. I never became as flamboyant as Cher, but *I learned a lot from her about being willing to express yourself with your personal style and letting yourself have a little fun with your appearance,* even if it's only your shoes, or your hair.

From Michael Eisner, *I learned that you have to feel free to fail, that you have to pitch every idea you've got and it doesn't matter if they're bad. Out of that freedom will come one great idea.* Never forget that Babe Ruth wasn't only the home-run champ. He was also the strike-out champ! *No risk, no gain.*

From Barry Diller, I learned that you can always do better, a proposition that had pros and cons for me. It reinforced, in a negative way, the whole perfectionistic obsession I had, but it also pushed me to where I never could have gone.

From Jeffrey, who was a brilliant executive even then, I learned what I called the "Jeffrey Katzenberg Theory of Getting Things Done," which is this: *If they throw you out the front door you go in the back door, and if they throw you out the back door you go in the window, and if they throw you out the window you go in the basement. And you don't ever take it personally.*

I learned, also, not to expect much in the way of praise from any of these men. I knew I'd scored with Simpson when occasionally he'd say, "Watch it, you're inching toward significance."

And I learned just by inhaling the atmosphere at Paramount. The competition was fierce and political, which was invigorating on one level, but deadly on another. I became wildly competitive. I felt threatened.

What I learned to do was to *focus on the work.* That's a very important lesson: *If you find yourself in a situation in which you feel competitive, focus on your work, focus on doing the best work you can do.*

Jeffrey was the most notorious workaholic in our group of notorious workaholics. And he was fearless about asking questions. I used to see him listening to Michael talk to filmmakers, watching Michael tear apart a script or a movie and put it back together again, improved. I used to see him running in and out of Dick Zimbert's office, asking the head of business affairs to explain the complicated details of a particular negotiation.

Working and networking were so important to Jeffrey that he had devised elaborate and impressive systems for every aspect of the Hollywood executive's responsibilities.

For instance, there was the fabled Katzenberg phone system. Jeffrey had an incredibly complex system of rotation, whereby the top two hundred people in his sphere were called, regularly, once a week or once every two weeks. (What was amazing about it was that, in those days before computers, it was manual!) These calls provided him with an extraordinary amount of information about who was making what movies with whom and which scripts were worth reading, and who was doing what to whom and how.

What was also important here was that there were two hundred people who truly felt they had an intimate relationship with Jeffrey Katzenberg.

I'd been in the job almost two years when Simpson stepped down, and Jeffrey became my immediate boss. So it was to him I went, with much trepidation, with my list of complaints. These ran the gamut from moans about what meetings I wasn't invited to, why I couldn't go on the company plane, what movies they wouldn't let me work on, to why I wasn't making as much money as my counterparts around town.

Was it because I was a girl? Nah. . . .

These complaints would build up over a period of time. As they occurred to me, I would write them down on a "buck slip"—a rectangular piece of heavy paper that bears the studio's logo on top and your name on the bottom. No mere piece of stationery, at the level I was at, the buck slip was a status symbol. When several of these buck slips had been filled up and piled up, I would march myself into Jeffrey's office, whip them out and say, "We have to talk."

I'd been doing this for some time when Jeffrey opened a drawer in the credenza behind him and said, "Let me show you something." And he fanned out his own collection of buck slips with the very same complaints. Only his were addressed to Don Simpson and Michael Eisner.

I wonder if Michael Eisner ever had buck slips intended for Barry Diller. . . .

This aggressive and highly energized gang also offered unique opportunities for understanding how good team play works. One of the most important corporate management lessons I got from Team Paramount is this: *Take care of the inside people first.* At one point there was a situation on *Young Sherlock Holmes* in which I was spending so much time trying to make the producer, Steven Spielberg, happy that once Michael Eisner asked me to do something and I didn't do it. I caught myself just in time, and it reinforced the importance of this idea: *First take care of the tasks that the boss needs done. Always.*

Some of the lessons were hard lessons. For example: I learned that *it's dangerous to follow orders without questioning them*. I got to learn that lesson twice, in the worst way.

Once, Frank Mancuso had me tell Steven Spielberg that the release of his movie would be on such and such a date. And, of course, when I did, Spielberg immediately said, "Who are you to tell me what the release date is?" Clearly, Mancuso had sent me to the wolves and I was too stupid to know it.

The other time, I got into a lot of trouble because I followed an "unbreakable" rule at Paramount, which was that if there's no signed actors' contracts the actors don't get on the set; they don't even get on planes to go on location. It's a big deal because after an actor's already started shooting the movie, he's—theoretically—in the position to demand a lot more money. What are you going to do if you've already shot a week's worth of film?

So I had Michael Keaton pulled off a plane. He was on his way to Venezuela to shoot *Gung Ho,* but he hadn't signed his contract yet. I was ordered to rush the contract to the airport and get him off the plane to sign it.

He got off the plane, but the contract didn't make it to the airport on time. The flight left without him.

Contract signed, he finally got to Venezuela, but he'd been extremely humiliated by our stupid maneuver. It took Michael and I seven years to have any kind of relationship after that. He was right and I was wrong.

* * *

Some of the lessons I learned were very bitter ones. There was a lot of pain and humiliation in those years. I wasn't the only one: that was the law of the Paramount land. Ned Tanen, who would later become president of Paramount's motion picture group, was quoted in *The New York Times* recently as saying, "This is a business where people wish you well only if they know you are terminally ill."

Hollywood is full of heartbreaks. It's not just the artists who suffer from rejection and mortification. I was often discouraged and dejected. I would walk into my office and I would close the door and I would say, "I won't cry, I won't cry, I won't cry." At the time I believed that—particularly if you were a woman— you could not cry. We were in corporate America. Crying was inappropriate. Of course, I knew that some women did it all the time, but I wasn't going to do it. At least, I wasn't going to let them see me cry.

It was in this period that I began to learn some important lessons about working with other women. At first I was always the only woman in a room; I got used to it and, mostly, I liked it. But when I look back I see the cost of that: it made me too competitive with other women.

It was a tough balancing act, being a woman in that place, and gauging how to juggle my masculine side and my feminine side. And it's interesting to see where the lines had to be drawn. In your dress, in your talk, in your body language, for starters.

I had to learn that *it's important to have a demarcation between your work and your personal life.* Not that I had a personal life then, but I was just beginning to glimpse what all this integration was about. I once heard a pop psychologist named Pat Allen speak and

she said, "Ladies, leave your balls in the office."
Remember that one.

At that moment, it was a moot point because there
was no difference between my office and my home. I
went out with a few men but no relationship bloomed.
In those days the thing to do was to hang around in
packs and go to parties and screenings together.
Business and personal were completely blurred. There
were no demarcations. The parties were really about
the same things as the office: work and power. Not
about sex. Everything was about work, work, work.
Ambition and work. It's funny because I often hear
people talk about Hollywood as this place where
there's always been an incredible amount of sex and
drugs, but that really was not my experience of it at all
in those years, the late seventies and early to mid
eighties. We worked very long hours, and I didn't see a
lot of drug-taking.

Every once in a while you'd be somewhere and
someone would disappear into a bathroom, but it was
fairly discreet. There were one or two notorious coke
habits, but there really wasn't one huge drug party all
the time. Or if there was, I wasn't invited to it. The
people I hung out with were just totally focused on
work, ambition and the status hierarchy of the studios.

Even before I formally met Barry Diller I was
already obsessed by him. He was clearly a brilliant
and visionary man. As head of ABC programming, he
invented both the movie of the week and the
miniseries. And now, here he was in the flesh. Diller

fascinates people. You can't get what he's like from photographs. In the flesh, he was power incarnate. He was the sexiest man I'd ever met.

I wanted to be him. Many women want to be with these men, but I wanted to be him. And it wasn't until I went to Columbia that I let go of wanting to be Barry Diller, or anyone else.

It's perhaps not so surprising that I wound up being obsessed by Barry Diller for years. I was totally ripe for this kind of idealization. The fact that there was no really interesting love in my life meant that someone like Diller could reign uncontested in my psyche. By then I was completely estranged from my parents. I had very few friends. I was hungry for engagement, for connection.

For years I dreamed about Diller. He handled power differently from anyone I've ever known, in this very complex, sexual way. His voice boomed. You couldn't not look at him. You couldn't help but be engaged by him. He had fantastic personal power. Nothing anyone ever did was good enough for him. Consequently, he pushed you into finding out how good you were. It was a very familiar feeling for me.

We were all intimidated by the collective power of Michael Eisner and Barry Diller. We would see them in the commissary or the parking lot and we'd be panting like dogs, like, Oh, please just recognize me. It was a very big deal if they did.

Barry Diller was larger than life and I cast a mythic mantle over him. When I became more competent, the balance changed and a lot of my fascination subsided. We became social friends because we were single and hung around with the same sort of group, and I got less intimidated. It's a testimony to Barry

Diller's tremendous charisma that he remained a powerfully erotic figure to me.

Finally, I proved an apt enough student at Paramount that I was given the tasks that traditionally go to the low man on the totem pole. The first production job I had to learn was to do script notes. In the development process, after the studio executives finish reading the script, they critique everything that they don't like about it, what doesn't work and why.

They want me to WRITE! I silently howled to myself. Even as a sportswriter, I'd been blocked by the need to be perfect. Each sentence had to be rewritten a hundred times. Now I had to write script notes that would be given to professional writers?!

Then I sat with Jeffrey as he went through movies, reel by reel, as we had for *Going Ape!* I would go with him to the dailies, to watch the film that had been shot the day before. Jeffrey would tell the filmmakers—the producer, director, writer, any combination—how he thought he could improve it. It was a lot of common sense and instincts. Did the performance work? Was it real? What did it look like? Was it in focus? Were the characters likable? Did the story work? Are there any plot holes? Did you care about the people?

I figured I could do that.

Eventually, I moved on to working on movies by myself. I was still reporting to other people, but my job had progressed beyond taking notes. My first project was with Richard Pryor. I worked with him on *Some Kind of Hero,* which was his first film after his accident. I was on my way.

I had learned. I'd learned seemingly small things: *To never use the word "I"; to always use the word "we," to be part of a team.* And I learned big things: *Don't ever be arrogant in success*—people will want to shoot you down. *And don't expect love from your bosses. You'll be disappointed.*

9

YOU
CAN MAKE
THAT CALL

1981. SANDRA DAY O'CONNOR IS THE FIRST WOMAN
named to the Supreme Court. The Supreme Court
upholds the law making statutory rape a crime for
men but not women. Reagan is wounded by a would-
be assassin. Mao's widow is given the death sentence
in China. Charles and Diana wed. Oxford gets its first
woman coxswain. Jean Harris murders Dr. Herman
Tarnower. The top songs of the year are sung by
women: "Physical," by Olivia Newton-John; "Bette
Davis Eyes," by Kim Carnes; and "Endless Love," by
Diana Ross and Lionel Richie. The big movies are
Raiders of the Lost Ark, Chariots of Fire, Reds and *On
Golden Pond.*

Now I had to get my own movies made. I needed to
find a great story idea. At Paramount, the idea was the
thing.

135

But no one was submitting scripts to me. In Hollywood, in production, your power would be measured by how many calls you get a day from agents, directors, actors, producers and writers. If you get hundreds of calls a day, you're powerful. Nobody was calling me. I'd done enough tagging after other people, I decided. I had to build my own relationships with agents and directors and writers. By and large, it was the agents who controlled the scripts that were out there in the marketplace. And I needed to get to know some directors, because you had to attract the right director to get your movie made. And without writers you have no scripts. The time had come to make some calls. The only problem was, I was convinced no one would call me back.

I realized how serious a problem this had become for me when I found myself wanting to call a talented actor-turned-director, Tony Bill, who had just done a wonderful movie called *My Bodyguard*. I wanted to ask him if he would have lunch with me. But I was nervous.

Jeffrey wasn't afraid. He would call anyone. He would call people for lunch he wanted to be in business with, people who were more powerful than he was. For instance, at the time, Sue Mengers was a legendary agent in town. If you wanted a star, you were pretty much obliged to go to her, because she represented people like Barbra Streisand, Burt Reynolds, Diana Ross, Gene Hackman and Michael Caine. Sue Mengers was a superstar in her own right. She wore muumuus and caftans and she would blow into the "in" restaurants and screenings on the arm of some star like some great ship under sail. And she had great shoes. She was one of the first really powerful women in this town and Jeffrey was dying to have lunch with her. It would be a great feather in his cap. But he wasn't important enough for her to spend two hours at lunch with.

So he kept calling her and she kept ignoring him. She wouldn't call him back. She wouldn't allow her secretary to make a lunch date with him. But Katzenberg would not take no for an answer and he kept calling her until she finally did have lunch with him.

Perseverance keeps popping up, doesn't it? It's one of the reasons he now runs the Walt Disney Studios.

I did develop my own strategy. I would go into my office and say to myself: "Pick up that phone. *Make the call*. Just make the call."

Sometimes I still do it. I still sit there and say to myself, "You can make the call." I've gone far in the movie business, but no matter how far I go, every time I pick up the phone to call Tom Hanks or Robin Williams, I wonder if they'll call me back.

And you know what? Sometimes they do and sometimes they don't. But it isn't about me. A really hard lesson to learn is that most of the time, *it's not about you*.

But what's most important, in this particular situation, is not what you feel but what you do. You can be afraid and still make the call.

I called Tony Bill. He called back. I had lunch with him, the first director I ever met on my own. He treated me like a person.

How do you talk to a director? I wondered. What I found out was it's just like talking to anyone. You talk about ideas. You talk about material, you talk about the movies you've both seen that you love, you talk about short stories that you might want to turn into movies. In talking about ideas, patterns of what you have in common begin to emerge and that gives you a way to work together. It's that common ground that relationships are built on.

I never got Tony Bill to direct anything, but we developed a relationship of mutual respect. I was and am really glad I made that call!

For all of the passionate brashness they had in common, the members of Team Paramount had very different styles. Barry Diller always wore the same thing: white handmade shirts of the sheerest cotton under a beige suit; he had suits in many different shades of beige. Michael Eisner was more loosely tailored. His suits were dark and not high fashion and he was more preppy. Don Simpson was very trendy. He was wearing a biker jacket and motorcycle boots before Dennis Hopper. Jeffrey wore slacks and an alligator shirt. He just didn't care. It was inefficient to spend time thinking about what he wanted to wear.

But they were a great group and many junior executives like me were inspired by their energy and their solidarity. There was a lot of talk in those days about Team Paramount. I was glad to be part of it, though always worried about my place in it. A lot of people didn't make it in the group or fell by the wayside.

Being funny was as important as having good ideas.

Everyone at Paramount was familiar with each senior executive's brand of humor. Barry had a caustic, very droll sense of humor. Don's was very dark. Michael's humor was playful. Jeffrey was a prankster.

Even as a junior executive, I knew that the quality of humor was a prerequisite for doing the job. That kind of pressure, I could handle.

But there was that gender thing.

For example, Jeffrey organized a raft trip every year. It was all men; actors, writers and agents and directors —and these were always the most interesting men. One year Tom Cruise went. I was desperate. Forget the fact that enormous amounts of business got done on that trip, these guys had a ball! And I kept saying, "I want to go," and Jeffrey would say, "No girls. Nooooo girls." They never did let me go.

So I knew I had to improve my status, and in a hurry, if I was going to stay in the game and not on the sidelines. Bringing in my own movie was now crucial. In eighteen months, I had not found a script I loved and wanted to make.

One day, I came back from lunch and there was only one name on my call list. The call was from Melinda Jason, a young agent in town whose calls no one returned in those days. But since nobody was calling me either, I called her back.

Melinda Jason was the agent for a writer named Tom Hedley, who had written a script. "It's a very hot script," she said. "It's probably not going to get made at Universal, but it's not quite in turnaround yet." Turnaround, I had learned, is when a movie gets canceled by one studio and is available to be picked up by another. "You have to read it and tell me if you like it," she said, "so that I can get them to put it in turnaround. The problem is, it's so secret I can't let you keep it. You'll have to read it and give it right back."

It was the High Holy Days and Melinda was having Yom Kippur break-the-fast dinner that evening at her mother's house. I, of course, was sans family. She said I could park my car in front of her mother's house and read the script in my car so I could give it right back. I sat outside her house in my red Fiat reading the script with a cigarette lighter. It was called *Flashdance*.

My friend producer Howard Rosenman *(Father of the Bride)* told me recently that when he interviews newcomers who want to get into the movie business, he always tells them the story of me reading the script in the car and then asks: "Do you have that kind of passion and tenacity?" It makes me laugh. I did it because I was convinced this was the way it worked. Who knew?

I loved this script. It was the story of a young girl who works as a welder. She does sexy dancing at night in a club but doesn't feel entitled to anything better.

She was me. I totally identified. Not with the sexy dancing, but I had always seen myself as the underdog. Rocky was an underdog and the way I saw *Flashdance* was *Rocky* with a female underdog. What this movie said was that if you want something badly enough, you can have it. I felt so in synch with this story that it was really the beginning of a lifelong obsession with movie underdogs.

I saw the movie in my head. I saw the movie on the

screen. I knew how to make the movie, even though I didn't know how to make movies. I could smell a hit. I felt in my gut that if I loved this story, audiences would love this story. I had never felt so sure about anything in my life. This was the first time I trusted my instincts completely.

The lesson here was that what was true in the movie was true in real life: *If you don't gamble on your instincts, nobody else will.* I was determined to get this movie made. The story had been developed at an independent production company called PolyGram, where Hedley had brought the germ of an idea based on something he'd seen about hard hat working girls doing strip dancing in bars in Toronto. It turned out that Lynda Obst, a woman I'd met at a dinner party a few months earlier, was the junior producer who had grabbed Hedley's idea and started developing it. She'd just moved from New York to get into movies and *Flashdance* was the first story she'd found that she liked, too. Lynda liked my street smarts, I liked her intellectual smarts. We both loved *Flashdance.* Jon Peters (always described as the hairdresser-turned-producer who'd been Barbra Streisand's boyfriend) and Peter Guber (ex-studio exec turned producer who is now chairman of Sony Pictures) had become partners at PolyGram and had decided to produce it.

I needed to convince Jeffrey and Don that we had to get it for Paramount. Diller, Eisner, Simpson and Katzenberg had been drilling into my brain that to get movies made you had to have three things: A good idea. Passion. And perseverance.

Eisner, especially, believed that the idea was the thing. That if it was good—and, most importantly, clear to the public—the movie could work. An idea that is accessible to people can usually be marketed.

Now I had to follow Diller's dictum, the most important lesson I learned from him, which is that *passion is the key to success.* He would say: "If you have enough passion to get up on top of this table and tell me why I should make this movie, then chances are I'm going to make this movie." His attitude was that the process of making a movie—starting with an idea and surviving through development, through production, and through release—could take years. And if you weren't completely passionate at the very beginning of the process, you weren't going to give a damn at the end of the process. A bored executive was going to make boring movies. And Barry Diller didn't like to be bored.

I wasn't even at the right level to make a movie. Not high enough yet. But I did have the passion, and now I had the idea. I had to sell them *Flashdance.*

Not easy, this crowd. These were the Killer Dillers. Most of them would go on to run their own studios. This was the ultimate training ground for tough. They should have issued helmets. I remember Don Simpson, wild, furry-bearded and outrageous, saying things like "I'm looking for commando players who can get behind enemy lines and get it done." (In fact, he had a subscription to *Soldier of Fortune* magazine at the time.)

Actually, Paramount, in some ways, was like being in the military. Diller was our general. He was out to break the agents' hold on Hollywood. He refused to sit around waiting for agents to sell him packages that already came with a script, an actor and a director. By and large, movies were much more expensive that

My dad, the "Man of Steel," with Mom on top, 1943.

At age two with my mother. Check out her outfit; she always had such style.

At five years old with my best friend, my three-year-old brother, Larry.

I always wanted to be one of the boys. And at this birthday party, I fit right in.

Still in my boy phase a year later, that's me on the left, the only girl in pants with my sailor's outfit on.

At age seven with Larry. My ugly period. I was so ugly it was mind-boggling. My mother kept telling me I'd grow out of it.

With my devoted grandparents, Nathan and Rebecca, who held hands for sixty years.

3

I've always liked this picture. It's also probably the last time my bare arm will ever be photographed.

Atlantic Beach Day Camp 1956

That's me, third from the left in high school as the infamous Kiltie. This is pre-kickline, when my kilt was still where it was supposed to be.

1964: My Great Neck South Senior High School graduation picture.

1979: My first publicity shot in the movie business. Long hair, long nails.

On the set of *Going Ape* with the first actor I'd met whose hair rivaled my own.

1980: With one of my favorite people, Richard Pryor, on the set of *Some Kind of Hero.*

The adventure continues. On the set of *Star Trek III: The Search for Spock* with Leonard Nimoy and Frank Mancuso.

1983: *The King of Comedy* opened the Cannes Film Festival. I was in heaven with (left to right) Jerry Lewis, Robert De Niro, and Martin Scorsese.

With Martin Scorsese in Tunisia, location-scouting for *The Last Temptation of Christ*. Those high heels are proof positive that even in the desert I wasn't secure enough to wear flats.

May 30, 1985,
my wedding day.

On the set of *Top Gun* with Tom Cruise. Oooh, what a
smile! Tom's isn't too bad, either.

8

Comparing bellies with Debra Winger at Paramount's seventy-fifth-anniversary party.

Barbra Streisand with my daughter, Rebecca.

Sure . . . I just threw Rebecca over my shoulder and did it all. Oh, if it were only that easy. . . .

1988: At the premiere of the restoration of *Lawrence of Arabia,* one of the projects I'm still most proud of (left to right): Freddie Young, director of photography; Steven Spielberg; Anne V. Coates, editor; Omar Sharif; Robert A. Harris, restorer; Jim Painten, restorer; Martin Scorsese; me; Peter O'Toole; and Sir David Lean.

Lawrence of Arabia was one of my favorite films, so when I met David Lean, I have to admit I was star-struck.

1989: With Jane Fonda at the *Old Gringo* premiere.

For convincing Cher to attend a charity bowling event, I was given a trophy for the person "most likely to be asked back."

1989: Being goosed by Bill Murray was one of the highlights of my Columbia years (Dan Aykroyd on the right).

David Geffen (left) and Victor Kaufman certainly contributed to my Hollywood education . . . big time!

1989: On the set of *Postcards from the Edge* with (left to right) John Calley, Carrie Fisher, and Mike Nichols.

If I didn't have such a great husband ... Michael Douglas is not just a pretty face. He's one of the smartest people I know.

With friends, producer Lynda Obst (left) and agent Ron Meyer (right) when I was given the Crystal Award by Women in Film.

14

Barry Diller pushed me further than I thought I could ever go.

My parents, Lillian and Nat. You can see where I got my hair.

Jodie Fisher (left) and Madonna cheered me on when I won the Crystal Award.

I was a co-host at this first Los Angeles luncheon for Hillary Rodham Clinton in 1992. That's my husband, Chuck, on the right.

Donald Duck passionately welcoming me to the *Aladdin* premiere on the Walt Disney lot. You haven't lived until you've french-kissed a duck.

way, to say nothing of the fact that you didn't get to choose the combination of talent you wanted to work with. Under Diller, Paramount developed its own movies, created its own packages. It was our responsibility to get our own ideas and develop them.

But once you had an idea, you had to convince your own side to go for it. At the time I didn't know how unique this way of doing things was. I thought all studio executives stood on tables and screamed.

Diller's Aggressive Advocacy and Yelling System became legendary, partly because the press got a big kick out of it. Aaron Latham, who probably coined the phrase "Killer Dillers," wrote aptly in *Manhattan, Inc.* that "Barry Diller taught his proteges to bite, kick, and yell. Now they're running Hollywood."

In retrospect I see that this was a tough education. I couldn't have endured it if I hadn't been a certain kind of person already, but it also marked me forever as someone who was willing to take the heat no matter what. This is an important lesson: *You need to be willing to take the heat . . . You need to take responsibility for your actions in business.* In my case that meant if I managed to convince Barry Diller and Michael Eisner to make a movie, then it was my responsibility to make it work. If it didn't, that was my responsibility, too. I had to own it, win or lose. *If you make a mistake, by the way, say, "I made a mistake, so kill me." But don't make excuses, don't try to cover it up, own up to it. If you admit to your mistake, it ends the conversation. If you try to cover it up, it extends it. It is respectable to say "I screwed up . . . I did it."*

* * *

Around this time, I was befriended by David Geffen, the visionary entrepreneur and brilliant mogul behind Geffen Records and the Geffen Film Company who has been so much in the news lately as a good friend of the Clinton administration. David was Barry Diller's best friend. It was amazing to me that someone with so much more success than I had would want to become friends with me. But David decided that he liked me and wanted to be in my life, and where I was on the food chain didn't matter to him at all. He befriends people he finds to be smart, or on a road that appeals to him. It doesn't matter what level they are at. He liked hanging around with me and I had a ball with him. He is intensely loyal to his friends. *The thing about David that is so extraordinary is that the concept of "no" is truly incomprehensible to him; I learned that lesson from him.*

Not only did David befriend me at that time, but he also befriended Jeffrey Katzenberg. These two are probably inseparable today, and they have a relationship as peers, but Jeffrey was not David's peer when their relationship started. David is simply not a snob. He's open-minded. He doesn't cocoon himself in a cage with "like animals."

Barry and David's other close friend was Sandy Gallin, a personal manager whose clients include Michael Jackson, Dolly Parton and Neil Diamond. I went almost everywhere with them. I couldn't figure out why they would befriend me, but they were insistent about it and to this day have never backed off that friendship.

I owe David Geffen big, with regard to my growing self-awareness at the time. One night we were having dinner and in the course of talking about something or other, he said, "Angry people like us . . ."

And I thought, "What is he talking about? I'm not angry." I kept thinking about it, though. I couldn't get the phrase out of my mind: "Angry people like us . . ." Finally, I realized that I wasn't angry. I was furious.

This was the beginning of my realization of how much work I had to do on myself. It wasn't until I lost my compulsive, previously unacknowledged rage that I really started to grow up.

Learning how to make deals was, of course, a crucial professional evolution, and I had some of the best teachers in the business. I still remember many of Dick Zimbert's lessons. Dick was head of business affairs, and then he was corporate counsel, but he was always my friend and teacher. Michael and Barry would not make a legal decision without consulting Dick Zimbert. They respected him enormously.

Dick was wonderfully droll. He was sometimes said to be the only one who understood the concept "rolling break-even." No one knew what it meant. Dick once said it must have been devised to confuse agents and entertainment industry lawyers with whom he sparred all the time. He would come up with this incredibly complicated formula for defining break-even, where the studio would kick in and where the talent participants would kick in. And I promise you that most of the people who were negotiating rolling break-even had no idea what it meant.

To learn how to make deals, I went to Dick Zimbert's office and asked, "What does net mean? What does gross mean in this contract? What is rolling break-even?" Eventually, Dick helped me realize that I could convert everything to net, which was much less complicated than trying to work out all these different formulas for gross.

That's the system I wound up sticking with. It doesn't mean that it's right or wrong, but it worked for me to simplify the terms. *I prefer to understand the conceptual point of view of a deal, not necessarily how you do the calculations.* Which makes sense since I flunked calculus twice. You can have a computer do that. Conceptually, do you want to give a director 10 percent of the pie? That was the way Dick suggested that I learn these things and that system has worked for me ever since.

But the most important thing to remember about a deal, and about negotiation, is that it is all about appetite. It's not the details or the complications of a deal that matter, it's how much you want it, and how much you're willing to spend for it. It's really simple.

So if you want to make a deal with Tom Cruise, you have to have a number in your mind. I don't care if it's a movie or a widget. How much do you want to make it for? How much is Tom Cruise worth in that particular movie? Is it a commercial premise or an arty premise? How much box office do you think you can achieve with this movie? Once you figure out your educated guess for what you might make, you can figure out how much appetite you are entitled to have.

Deal-making is not so much about negotiation as it is about putting a price on your appetite and then sticking to it in every deal.

You can't let your competition sway you. One of the most important things I learned is that you must be willing not to get it. You must be willing to let go. Then it will come back to you.

If you're negotiating from a place of desperation, you're dead. You're not clear and you're not objective.

Set your boundaries ahead of time. Set your appetite ahead of time. Then be ready to let go.

I never lost a star I wanted to work with because of a problem in the deal. There were stars I didn't get because they didn't want to do the movies I wanted to do. And I may have lost someone because I didn't have an appetite. But I never lost someone because of a deal.

Now I had to pitch *Flashdance*.

It was time to put to use some of the lessons I had been learning. I got myself together and strode into the production meeting. I began, *"Flashdance is a female Rocky."*

Jeffrey bought in. But I had a lot of work to do on the rest of Team Paramount.

At first, Simpson, who had become president of production, paid no attention to me. He had a lot on his mind and I was low on the totem pole. Not only couldn't I get him to buy into my dream, I couldn't get him to buy into me. Since he was my immediate boss, there was no way I was going to get a green light for *Flashdance* if he didn't go for it.

On top of that, what was also complicating my life was this phenomenon of roaming men. By habit, these guys wandered in and out of each other's offices. By the time they got to the weekly production meeting, all the really important decisions had already been made. Big decisions, like who would direct, and who would star. I did not participate in these ad hoc meetings because I was not part of this herd of roaming men. The lesson here? *Don't wait for an invitation. When you have an opinion or an agenda, don't wait for the scheduled meeting. One on one is a much more effective way of getting something done.* Join the roamers.

So here I was, marooned in my own office, and I couldn't even get them to read *Flashdance,* I couldn't get them to pay any attention to it.

I began to despair. One day I went down to talk about it with one of my mentors, Paramount's chief financial officer, Art Barron, a delightful, cherubic man with a very quick wit and a habit of mumbling, so that you'd have to get really close to hear what he was saying. I adored him.

"Are you unhappy?" Art Barron asked me.

"Yes," I said.

"Could it get any worse?" he asked.

"No," I said.

"Quit," said Barron.

"What do you mean, quit?"

He said, "Quit. What do you have to lose?"

"Nothing," I said.

He spoke quietly. Art Barron always spoke in this very, very quiet voice. But I heard him.

That night, I had dinner with Simpson at Le Dome and told him I was leaving. I said to him, "If you don't want to make this movie, you'll never want to make any movie that I ever want to make."

"What movie?" he said.

148

He paid attention to me for the first time and heard me out. Now, I don't think he supported the movie because I threatened to quit. I think he wanted to make the movie because he thought it was a good idea. But I did make him pay attention to me. The squeaky wheel theory. He just needed a push.

Shortly afterward, Simpson resigned to become an independent producer and went into partnership with Jerry Bruckheimer, who had produced *American Gigolo* and *Cat People*. Paramount asked them if they would produce *Flashdance* and they agreed to take it on as their first project. In April, we hired a new writer, a very experienced and pricey writer named Joe Eszterhas (who would later write *Basic Instinct*), to root the story, which had been somewhat dreamy in Hedley's script, in blue-collar reality.

But then twenty-seven directors turned it down. It was crushing. This was rejection on a scale I could never have imagined, and I took each and every one personally because I thought this movie was about me, the fish out of water. How many times could I pull myself up and bob back to the surface?

It was Jeffrey who saved me again. *"Don't take rejection personally,"* he kept saying, and then he'd tell me again how if he knocked on the front door and they didn't open the door, he walked around the back and went into the back door, and if they didn't open the back door, he crawled into the basement. Not taking rejection personally was one of the hardest lessons for me. I'd be okay for a bit and then I'd get chipped away at and would go back to taking it personally. "You can't let it get to you," Joel Silver would lecture me. "Our business is all about self-respect, and no one's going to give that to you. *As long as you believe in yourself, you win.* It doesn't matter what anyone else does."

From everything that's known about successful people, rejection is seen as just another experience, an experience that can't interfere with your sense of mission. I was never as good at it as some of my colleagues, but I became good enough at enduring the feelings I had, which is the next best thing.

Everyone who stays in the ring learns that lesson sooner or later. Everyone. Not long ago, I saw then governor Bill Clinton at a fund-raiser. It was right after the New Hampshire primary, where he had taken some serious blows. I had been working for him for about six months by then so I felt comfortable enough to say: "You're like a bop bag. They punch you. You come up. They punch you again and you come up again. You really take punches well."

He smiled and seemed pleased and wandered off to shake some more hands. An hour later, he got back around to me. He said: "You know, I'm really glad you pointed that out to me. I do take a good punch, don't I?"

The bop bag strategy certainly worked for Jeffrey. Diller and Eisner appointed him as head of production to succeed Don Simpson. He saw what I saw in *Flashdance* and, with his help, I didn't give up.

I knew Adrian Lyne was the right director for this movie. He had made one previous movie, *Foxes*. I had also seen a reel of his commercials, and I'd been really impressed. It had occurred to me that he could use the same techniques for what I now thought of as "my" movie. One of the reasons *Flashdance* succeeded is that it was the first movie that tied into the MTV style of cutting. It was fast, sweaty, sexy, and musically very hip.

For some reason, as inexperienced as I may have been, when I looked at Adrian Lyne's commercials I grasped that he understood the aesthetic of the newly emerged MTV generation. I had a sense of how he listened to music, how he saw women, and I knew this was the feel that would work for *Flashdance*.

He said no. So I worked on him. He said no again. So I took him to lunch at Le Dome. He said no. Le Dome was next to an elegant, very glossy lingerie shop. After lunch, I walked him into the shop and said, "Look, here's what the movie feels like."

It was an offer he could not refuse. In retrospect it seems to me that this gesture was on the money not just because I exploited his taste for sexy babes (you should see his wife, Sam . . .), but also because it must have ignited a spark in his mind, some image of the movie that excited him. Adrian is nothing if not visual. I kept talking to him about the story, about the girl. I understood her so well that I must have conveyed to him what she could mean to many other young women. He finally saw what this girl's dream was and how the audience could dream with her. He agreed to do the movie. I had a director.

Momentum was building. The script was out of Universal, at Paramount, and in development. Unfortunately, that didn't mean much in Hollywood. Studios develop 125 to 150 scripts a year. At that time, only 15 to 20 got made. The green light to get a movie made is the highest power in Hollywood and can only come from the very top. At Paramount, this was Diller and Eisner. Anyone can say "No."

Flashdance was brought to the table at a meeting in San Francisco of Bluhdorn, Diller, Eisner, and Katzenberg. As it happens, they needed product. They knew they had to move with blinding speed to fill a big gaping hole in the spring release schedule. *Flashdance* was one of the fillers. In the end they made this movie because they needed product, not because I threatened to quit.

But that's okay. Whatever works. . . .

We struck a deal to reimburse PolyGram for their development costs, and Guber and Peters pulled back to become executive producers on the project. This story had been around for four years. Now it was being raced to the screen. It was scheduled for an April 15 release. Here was my first movie, facing an impossible deadline. Shooting started October 18. It would wrap by December 30. It was September 1.

I had my first green light.

I was a member in good standing of Team Paramount. At a meeting not long afterward, Barry Diller said something about how extraordinary it was that occasionally even someone who is very low on the totem pole can get a movie made if they are passionate and tenacious enough. He had never seen it before, he said, but it had been done with *Flashdance.* It could be done. He was talking to the whole room but he was looking at me when he said it and I felt at last that he respected me.

I was on top of the world. Or so I thought.

I strapped myself in.

10

FLASHFIGHT

1981–1982. MAJOR RATINGS FOR CHARLES AND DIANA's royal wedding extravaganza on TV. For the first time in the rock era, the top two songs of the year are by female vocalists. The big movies are *Raiders of the Lost Ark, On Golden Pond, Arthur, E.T., Rocky III, An Officer and a Gentleman* and, yes, *Porky's*. Americans love *Tootsie*'s gender-bending humor.

What's the first thing you do when you get a green light on a movie? You worry.

Now that my project was finally in the works, my worries had only just begun.

Luckily, nobody knew. I was smart enough not to go around telling people: "I don't know anything, *and* I'm scared to death." Not even Adrian Lyne, the director, knew. We got along wonderfully together. We became friends and we were very much in synch with regard to the work, but he had no idea how anxious I was. I'd make sure I began my sentences with "I don't know anything but I think . . ." And I'd never talk about how I felt. In these situations others are so busy dealing with their own fear, insecurities and the problems they have to solve that they don't have enough energy left to notice you're shaking with terror yourself.

The challenges that had to be met were truly formidable. To begin with, the story was insane. Think of it, a welder who wants to be a ballet dancer? It was crazy, though frankly, I wasn't aware of that. I mean, people told me afterwards that it was a ludicrous script, but I loved it. What did I know? And, by the way, what I've come to learn is that if you ask ten people to read a script you're going to get ten different reactions to it.

In the words of screenwriter extraordinaire William Goldman, "Nobody knows anything."

Sometimes I ask myself what I would do today if someone came into my office and pitched a movie about a welder who wants to become a ballerina. I don't know. But I did know that that character was me, and that's what enabled me to understand the dynamic of that story. But that also added tremendous pressure and weird psychological baggage to the project.

So, in every way, I had too much at stake here.

In addition, there were too many cooks stirring this broth, and they weren't about to take instructions, at least not gracefully, from the little Paramount *pisher* whose first movie this was. There were so many people at the helm of this movie that even now it boggles the mind to try to sort them out. In fact, after the movie came out and was a huge success, an article appeared in the *Los Angeles Times* called "Flashfight," in which the writer tried and failed to figure out who was entitled to what credit in relation to the movie. "There's a truism in Hollywood that success has a thousand fathers and failure is an orphan," Dale Pollock, the writer, pointed out. The roster of the people claiming credit was so long that they were listed in the article like characters in a play.

"It's the usual Hollywood debate when an unexpected success comes along to take in 52 million at the box office and launch hit records and fashion fads. In this case the battle behind the sets is especially confusing—because there are so many people claiming *Flashdance* as their own." Actually, Pollock was wrong. The film did over $90 million in the U.S. alone. And it sold over five million records. *Flashdance* wound up being a really big deal, generating huge profits for the company.

But I'm getting ahead of myself. A number of senior people at Paramount were involved with all the important decisions. During preproduction and production Jeffrey Katzenberg in particular was watching closely. But he was not alone. A list of the players I had to deal with on this, my first project, on the production team alone, would include people who became some of Hollywood's most successful and most notorious characters.

In part, this was because of this movie's complicated geological layers. Bear with me for a moment:

Bruckheimer had been the producer initially assigned by Paramount to the movie. He was joined by

Simpson when Simpson left as president of production at Paramount. Before the movie even got to Paramount, the original producers had been Jon Peters and Peter Guber, but they became executive producers when Bruckheimer and Simpson took over as producers. Still with me?

In fact, Jerry Bruckheimer and Don Simpson on the one hand, and Jon Peters and Peter Guber on the other, wound up being the two premier producing teams of the eighties. They were always in competition with each other, and that competition began with *Flashdance*. Simpson and Bruckheimer went on to produce *Beverly Hills Cop*, (and *Cop II*), *Top Gun* and *Days of Thunder*. Guber and Peters went on to produce *Batman, Rain Man* and *The Color Purple*, and to run Sony pictures.

There seemed to be no end to the conflicts these guys would get into, all of them designed to give me heart attacks. On the one hand you had Jon Peters taking credit for everything. On the other hand you had Don Simpson banning him from the set.

It was Lynda Obst who had developed *Flashdance* at the start. Lynda, who worked for Guber and Peters, went on to produce *The Fisher King* and *Sleepless in Seattle,* but at the time, she was just starting out too. Lynda was my opposite number. Just as I was struggling for turf and attention at Paramount, Lynda was Guber and Peters's development person and they weren't really paying that much attention to her either. We were sort of on a parallel course although she was in a production company and I was at a studio.

Naturally, we were very competitive. On Lynda's part there was a reluctance to deal with the fact that the movie she had developed was now my project. On my part I was less than compassionate and understanding of her position. And I was intimidated and jealous. She had come to L.A. from *The New York Times Magazine,* where she had been an editor, and I felt that she knew a lot of things and a lot of people I didn't know. Lynda is very educated, very literate, very smart, very articulate, and I didn't see myself as any of those things.

Eventually, we became very good friends and we've talked often about those *Flashdance* days and what happened to us. Lynda points out that we were made to feel that there weren't that many pieces of the pie for women. We felt more competitive with other women than we did with the men who bounded ahead of us without having to compete with us at all! It was a classic setup and we paid dearly for the lesson. In the course of making this movie we had many fights and there wound up being a great deal of bitterness about who did what and who was entitled to what credit. The lesson here is: *Other women are not the enemy . . . and neither are men. It's only about the work and how good your work is.*

The most miserable relationship I had in connection with *Flashdance* was the affair I had with the writer of the original screenplay, Tom Hedley. My relationship with him happened right at the beginning of my involvement with the project and ended six months later, but it left me as bruised as any relationship I've ever had with anyone, before or after.

To begin with, it's not a good idea to date people you work with. Trust me on this. There are the old jokes about women using sex to get ahead and sleeping their way to the top, but in my experience that's never what happens. *You can only sleep your way to the middle.* Not that this applied to my relationship with Tom Hedley, who was only trouble to me in any event.

In this case, it was also a disaster because the relationship itself was extremely sick. There were men I'd seen, but this was the first real relationship I had in Hollywood. While this was a monogamous affair for me, it wasn't for Hedley. And he was very passive-aggressive and withdrawn. I remember he always used to sit back. You know how people lean forward when they're talking to you? Tom would lean back instead, so that you'd have to incline even more towards him. Everything about him was like that.

In a way, Tom Hedley was the antithesis of me. He was incredibly "white bread," a classic, witty, hard-drinking *Esquire* journalist. He was very well educated and very literate. I was out there and very forthright, while he was withdrawn and uncommunicative. I was giving. He was not. The whole relationship was about seduction and manipulation and rejection. I was already terribly insecure in my professional life but this emotional abuse was more painful than anything else I'd experienced, unlike anything I'd ever known, and now my sexual self-confidence, which had always served me well, also deserted me.

I was in such bad shape I remember thinking, My career's over, because I'm never getting out of this bed again. The one really lucky thing about it is that it threw me back into therapy.

I had some effective short-term crisis therapy with a doctor named Tessa Warshaw, who was really helpful, but it soon became apparent that this was no short-term thing.

Looking back after all these years, along with my husband and my daughter, it's my therapist, Dee Barlow, whom I have to credit for a human connection that's enabled me to learn and grow and flower. But in those early days, it was really, really rough. Dee says she's never known another patient for whom therapy was as painful. It's as if I was so bruised there wasn't anywhere I could be touched that didn't hurt. I was incredibly lucky to find someone as gentle and smart and competent as she was.

Flashdance wasn't so much a job as a high-speed toboggan ride with ten other riders in which I often had to shut my eyes and just hope we'd all somehow get down to the bottom of the hill without killing ourselves or each other, or crashing. Every once in a while, I'd try to steer just a little.

My friend, the great producer Dan Melnick, once said that I was like a tank. I believe he said it while we were working on *Footloose,* which he produced, the movie I worked on immediately after *Flashdance,* and which I was developing all the while the *Flashdance* madness was going on. He said I was like a tank because once I set my sights on something I wanted I just put my head down and kept going, no matter what. The worse it got, the more I kept going.

Melnick was a really important friend in my life. He had very good advice to give, which he drew from invaluable experience. He had run two studios, Columbia and MGM, and at one point he was president of ABC. He is someone who is truly interested in other people and not threatened by ambitious young women. . . . (He was also Sherry Lansing's mentor.) The lesson there is that, *yes, there are men who stop us. But there are also, and gratefully so, men who feel and*

*act otherwise. There are men who feel invested in our
success and who will help us if we let them.*

The fact is that it had taken me so long to get
Flashdance made (actually, by Hollywood standards,
it really wasn't that long, but it had seemed like an
eternity to me), that once it happened I was like a dog
with a bone. I wasn't going to let go, no matter what.
For me, *Flashdance* was a "Flashfight" not just because of all the fighting and rivalry, professional,
corporate, sexual and God knows what else that went
into the making of it, but also because of my struggle
with myself to do my best.

But in 1982, while *Flashdance* was already in the
works, Barry Diller decided to build a new commissary. Beforehand, senior executives would get in their
cars and drive to the Polo Lounge in Beverly Hills for
breakfast, or Ma Maison or Le Dome for lunch. But
most of us either got a sandwich in or went to the little
coffee shops just outside the gates, Oblath's and
Nickodell's.

Now there was a place to meet on the lot, the
Paramount Cafe. It had no movie memorabilia, it was
a chic three-star restaurant, a place to have power
lunches. It dramatically changed the lot because people congregated there. It became a kind of meeting
room, a place where you could have executive break-
fasts and lunches and it brought the company together
in a familial way that hadn't existed. It got some of the
roaming men out of the halls and the offices and into
the open. There was a pecking order at the tables that
was, of course, endlessly fascinating to everyone.

Barry and Michael visibly held court at the far tables on the upper left and, believe me, everybody watched.

But what was more important for me is that they could see me too. Now all the breakfasting and lunching and dining I'd been doing all this time with agents and writers and actors and directors began to pay off. I was developing relationships with as much of the new talent in Hollywood as I could catch in my net. I would bring them to lunch at the Paramount Cafe. I'd come in with my hair, and my attitude, and my one Armani jacket I got on sale and I'd be having lunch with Sean Penn or Tom Cruise or Jim Brooks or Adrian Lyne or Michael Douglas. It gave me visibility.

I used my little bit of visibility and clout to play my hunches and I hit the mark enough times that it began to look as if my instincts would turn out to be as accurate in this domain as they had been in my previous enterprises.

For instance, as the third scriptwriter on *Flashdance,* I brought in Katherine Reback, who had written only one movie up until then. Hedley's script had been jettisoned very early on and Joe Eszterhas had been brought in (at a ransom fee of $200,000—he now gets $3 million) to rewrite it, but while Eszterhas had tremendously improved Hedley's version, it still wasn't there. Neither Hedley nor Eszterhas had made the girl in the movie or her emotions real. Neither of them had given her a voice and a dream to go with it. In Hedley's version she worked for the phone company and did sexy dancing at night. In Eszterhas's version she was a welder and that was an improvement, but it still wasn't it.

The fact that I had the nerve to even recommend

hiring Katherine still floors me. She'd never had a movie made. But the reason I hired her was that she had talent. I gave her first script, *The Receptionist,* to Simpson and he concurred.

Katherine and I had become friends and we always had these conversations like single women have. You know, as in:

"He'll call."

"No, he's not going to call."

"Yes, he will. He's going to call."

"No, I'm telling you, he's not going to call. He's never going to call me again."

"I'm telling you, he's going to call."

Which is how real people speak, real women. It's how we spoke. We wanted Jenny Beals's character, Alex, to have real conversations like these.

The official relationship between Katherine and me began one weekend when we both escaped to Palm Springs and were working on scripts by the pool. She writing one, me reading twelve. I handed her a script. "Please read this for me," I said, on instinct.

Katherine saw the problem right away. "She's this trashy dancer, but she doesn't want to be anything. What is this but Cinderella, abused, in the dirt, feeling unentitled to go to the ball? What would the equivalent dream be for this fish out of water?"

Katherine and I brainstormed all that weekend and we figured it out. Alex would want to be a real dancer, a ballerina. But she would not feel entitled to go to the ballet academy. She would go to apply and then be too intimidated. I loved the image of her big welder's boots among the ballet slippers. (Shoes again!)

Katherine had many great ideas. I remember the day I started feeling we were totally on track. It was when we got to the scene that became the crux of the movie, when Alex's best friend, Jeannie, the ice skater who fell in the rink during competition and didn't get up, whispers to Alex: "Remember at the tryouts . . . when I fell? I coulda gotten up. I didn't want to. I wanted to stay there. I just wanted to stay right there until . . . someone came along and carried me away." She wanted to be rescued. Now the entire movie hung on the question: Will Alex pick herself up and claim her dream? Will she dance her audition, and when she falls, will she get up? I knew how she felt.

I took Katherine to meet Don, Jerry and Adrian. I was as nervous and protective as a mother hen. In their usual fashions, Don grilled her, Jerry smiled and listened, and Adrian was ebullient. They talked out all the new story ideas and Katherine was hired on the spot. As I walked her out of the meeting, Don turned to her. "Congratulations," he said. And then, "You've got two weeks to write this movie." Good-bye, good luck and break a leg.

Great people worked on this movie. The costume designer Michael Kaplan, who created the *Flashdance* look with the torn sweatshirt, also worked on *Blade Runner*. Jeffrey Hornaday did the choreography, which really defined the attitude of the movie. It was so crucial that it functioned as an extra character. He went on to choreograph Madonna's Truth or Dare tour. Giorgio Moroder, who wrote the score, later worked on *Top Gun*. Phil Ramone was our musical coordinator and produced the record. He also is the one who found the spectacular break dancers. Phil already had a solid reputation as a producer. (He had worked with Billy Joel, among others.)

We had a great crew. Chemistry among the crew is

as important as chemistry among the actors. You have to cast the crew with as much attention as you cast actors.

Jenny Beals, who starred in the movie, was breathtakingly beautiful. We found her in a general casting call (usually referred to with the elegant phrase "cattle call") in Chicago at the point when we were taping auditions for hundreds of young women across the country.

Jenny was one of three finalists for the role of Alex. It had taken quite a lot of deliberation to get down to three, but now a decision had to be made. We screentested them. That's when we used the out-of-work Costner to feed the actresses their lines. The camera was aimed over his shoulder onto her face so that we almost never saw his face on screen. Only the back of his head.

Every once in a while there's a blatant reminder of what a men's town Hollywood is. Only men were invited to view these screen tests, which were henceforth known as the "peter meter" screenings. It was what you might call natural selection. That's how Jenny Beals got her part.

She and I wound up becoming friends, maybe from the day that I attended the very first wardrobe fitting which, for some reason, Jon Peters decided to attend. We hadn't seen much of him until then, but he wanted to be there during the wardrobe parade. I made sure I was there too. She got a chaperone and I got a friend.

I was very close to Don and Jerry. By then Don and I had a relationship in which Don would call me up about the script and we would have conversations that would go on for hours and hours into the night. Once we got finished talking about the script, I could talk about anything to him. He was magnetic and funny and incredibly seductive. I think his modus operandi was to seduce anyone he needed to seduce. This had to do with business and not necessarily with sex. It was in an intellectual context. The fact is that I was wildly attracted to him, and had been pretty much from the moment I met him. But he had about as much interest in me as he did in a kumquat.

And my hunch about Adrian Lyne totally panned out. He was the perfect director for this movie. (Later, he'd go on to make *Fatal Attraction* and *Indecent Proposal*.) Even then, Adrian was a great character: very English, puckish, bright and funny. He had a great sense of the moment he was in from a pop culture point of view and a very precise vision about how the movie should look.

The fact is that this movie had the right combination of people working on it and that's key. That's indispensable. But if all these people were so wonderful, why were there so many fights? Here's an example.

Adrian's work was very beautiful, visually. He had a number of signature details that had to do with how he lit his movies and how he framed his shots. One element that he was very fond of was smoke.

Now, there were two things that Michael Eisner hated in his movies: dust (so we never made any Westerns) and smoke.

So one day, Michael was watching dailies, and he said, "There's too much smoke in here and you can't see the people. It doesn't look real." (How real could it be, Michael? She's a ballet dancing welder . . .)

So I said to Don and Jerry, "Michael wants you to cut down the smoke."

The next day Michael watched dailies again and

there was no change in the quantity of smoke. He was getting angry. "You tell them to get rid of the smoke."

So this time I went to the set and I saw this big old smoke machine and I explained that Michael had said no smoke. "Please, no smoke. He's really mad. He gets really weird about this smoke thing."

So the next day, predictably, the Smoke Problem— as it became known—was as bad as it had been the day before. So this time I went back down there and I stood on the set and I saw to it that they used no smoke.

At some point in the afternoon, I went out to get a quick bite. When I came back I caught this guy running around the set with a little tin plate with a square thing sitting on it. He was blowing on it and enormous amounts of smoke were coming from the square thing.

A filmmaker will do anything to get what he wants. Adrian Lyne wanted smoke and no matter what Michael Eisner did, Adrian Lyne was going to have smoke. It's an image I still carry in my mind, that guy running around with the plate, blowing on it to make it smoke.

It wasn't all that funny. There were violent blowups too, and 99.9 percent of the time I lived in massive anxiety and free-floating exasperation. When principal photography started and I saw the very first dailies, I panicked.

I panicked because, even with all the smoke, Jenny's loft, the place where she lived in the movie, was a pigsty.

I took a deep breath and I went down to the set—the first time I dared to get involved in the actual production side—and I said to Adrian, Don and

Jerry, "This place is a pigsty. She wouldn't live like that. You've got to clean it up." Adrian was so angry, he said, "Since you know so much, show us. Show us exactly what you would do." He called my bluff: I had never been on a set, much less communicated with a production designer.

I took a deep breath and blurted, as fast as I could: "Wash the windows, clean the floors, replace the dead plant in the corner, and get rid of this cum-stained couch!" Oops. I could not believe I said that. But it broke the tension. They laughed. And they listened.

Finally, we showed a rough cut of the movie to my bosses at the studio. It was harrowing, just harrowing. I went back to Dan Melnick's office to cry. I didn't quite know what was wrong with the picture but no one was happy. By that point we were about to go into production with *Footloose* and I just couldn't shake my dread. Was I wrong about everything? Dan told me about Bob Fosse, whom he had worked with on *All That Jazz*, that every time he saw a rough cut, Fosse would go into the bathroom and throw up.

"So you're in good company," Dan said. "Calm down and let's think about what works and what doesn't work with your movie. Then you can throw up."

I was right, though, that not everyone had liked the movie. At this point Michael Eisner started to *potchkee* with it.

He had us reshoot the end so that it built to an exciting conclusion. In the last moments of the movie Jenny auditions for the snobs at the ballet school. We knew the audition dance had to be a show stopper. This is where movie magic comes in.

The best description of what happened next was

chronicled years later by Aaron Latham in the February, 1988, issue of *Manhattan, Inc.* He wrote:

As reshot, the closing number appears to be danced by Jennifer Beals, but it was actually performed by a troupe of specialists. The production team searched for the best leaper in the business and filmed her leaping—with such conviction that she broke her foot. They got the best pirouetter and shot her whirling on one leg. And they got the best break dancer and photographed him spinning on his back. He just happened to be not only male but also black. So they gave him a wig and light makeup and turned him into a "Jennifer Beals" who spun . . .

We wrapped on December 31. The movie was to come out in April. Now the fights over credit began.

Credit is a big deal in Hollywood, more than parking spaces and phone calls. So many people were starting out, in one way or another, on this movie that we all needed credit badly for our careers. Just as you might suspect, people lowest on the totem pole fared the worst. As the company executive, I got no screen credit; executives never get screen credit. However, I did get my share of recognition from my bosses within the company. Lynda Obst, who had found the script and had nursed it along for two years, was listed only as an associate producer, the lowest credit she could have received. Katherine Reback didn't get credit at all, even though she was on this project from September, 1982, until the day they wrapped the movie.

The fights were so outrageous that they made their way into the press. It makes good copy, I guess, to watch all these Hollywood people jockey for position and to make fun of them for trying to get their name on a picture and claim it. But there was a lot of real disappointment there. A lot of people worked really hard and did deserve some form of recognition.

Meanwhile, to show you just how much Paramount believed in the movie, they sold off 25 percent of it to a private investment firm as a hedge against losses—a few weeks before it opened. They wanted to cover themselves in case it bombed.

Well, you know the rest. This little movie with its $7 million budget wound up doing $90 million domestic box office. It started a ripped T-shirt craze, a dance craze, a workout craze; it spawned rock 'n' roll hits. In fact, we made a video for MTV of "What a Feeling," which was the beginning of movie marketing through MTV.

The critics hated it. No surprises there. It hurt me a lot but it was something I would have to get used to.

The great moment for me was when the movie opened, at the Village Theater in Westwood. Don, Jerry, Adrian and I were pacing in the back of the theater, watching the audience. We paced all day and all evening watching this movie over and over again. I'll never forget the manager, an incredibly nice man. He saw we were nervous and he kept bringing us popcorn and soda.

My moment—the moment that I'll always remember—is standing in back of the theater when, in the middle of the movie, an audience full of young girls stood up and began dancing in the aisles. I knew then that the movie worked, and that I'd participated in something that could make people feel transported. I think that is what hit me the hardest: how in two hours, a movie could have that kind of effect on its audience.

My brother called me that night from New York to tell me that he had seen the movie in a theater and that there had been a spontaneous standing ovation. They were standing up in New York. Wow. What a feeling. . . .

But I didn't get to feel good for long. That's the thing about the job. Very soon, I was already in over my head again with problems on *Footloose*. The lesson I was finally confident enough to learn, however, was that I could make jokes about some of the things that might once have embarrassed me.

For example, when Dean Pitchford, screenwriter and the man responsible for creating all the songs in the movie, and Craig Zadan, Melnick's coproducer, brought their music to my office, I had no tape deck in my office. I hadn't gotten high enough up on the perk ladder yet to merit one. So we all piled into my car to listen to the music on my car stereo.

And the problems that we had had on *Flashdance* came back to haunt us on the ending of *Footloose*. I remember the screening, attended by the director, the producers. Norah Kaye was there too, the great ballerina who was the wife and collaborator of Herbert Ross, the director of *Footloose*. (Herbert Ross also directed *Steel Magnolias, California Suite* and *The Goodbye Girl*.) Norah was a wonderful character, very elegant but very outspoken. She had previously been married to the concert violinist Isaac Stern, about whom she was known to complain in that nasal voice that all he did all day was "squeak, squeak, squeak" on his violin.

When the rough cut of *Footloose* was over, we all just sat there, sure that something was wrong, but not quite knowing what. Suddenly, Norah Kaye's inimitable nasal whine rang out: "Herbert, you old fart, you made a really good movie but the end sucks."

But never mind. By then the press had begun to call me "the mother of the modern movie musical." No kidding. A lot had changed. I had traveled a long distance. At this point, I remember telling my friend Margie over a dinner at Hamburger Hamlet that I no longer had time to confide in friends.

I had become an executive who could get a movie made. I had become a Killer Diller.

The songs from *Footloose* became big hits and, when we went platinum, Columbia Records gave a party for everyone who had worked on the movie.

Dan Melnick introduced me as the Paramount executive in charge of *Footloose* to Walter Yetnikoff, president of Columbia Records. Yetnikoff seemed quite willing to chat.

"Baby, do you know how I define success?" he asked.

"No," I said.

"By the size of my erection," said Mr. Yetnikoff.

Since I was never going to be able to measure my success his way, I knew I'd have to find my own way.

11

YOUPEOPLE

1983. SALLY RIDE IS THE FIRST AMERICAN WOMAN TO GO UP in space. Anchorwoman Christine Craft, who won a $500,000 suit for sex discrimination, sees the conviction overturned when a federal judge rules her employer was justified in firing her because viewers found her to be too informal in dress and manner, too opinionated, and "lacking warmth and comfort." The National Council of Churches issues a new Bible in which God is not referred to by gender and "man" is replaced by "humanity" or "humankind." The first compact discs are sold in record stores. The top songs are "Every Breath You Take," by The Police, "Flashdance . . . What a Feeling," by Irene Cara, "Say Say Say," by Paul McCartney and Michael Jackson and "Billie Jean," by Michael Jackson. The big movies are *Return of the Jedi, Terms of Endearment, Trading Places, Wargames, Superman III* and *Flashdance.*

* * *

In early 1983, two events took place on jet planes that rewrote the script of my career and of my love life. Flying back to the U.S. from the Dominican Republic on the Gulf & Western plane, Charlie Bluhdorn died of a heart attack. And on a flight to ShoWest in Las Vegas I met Martin Scorsese.

I was truly saddened by the death of Bluhdorn, who had meant so much to me. But *corporations don't mourn* and I knew that a new chairman would have to be named, sooner rather than later.

His name was Martin Davis. He was a man with a much more modern, streamlined corporate sensibility than Bluhdorn's. And, in fact, Wall Street loved Martin Davis because he took an unwieldy corporate empire and focused it on the entertainment business. The stock soared. But he still had a lot of problems to solve.

I had my own problems to solve when I got on a charter flight to Las Vegas to go to ShoWest, the big annual exhibitors' convention. Right before we left for the airport, Frank Mancuso, who had been promoted to president of the motion picture division and who was in charge of this convention, had told me I could not sit on the dais. There was no room for me.

Now I have to tell you that for a young Hollywood executive on her way up, this is actually worse than not having your own parking space. The seating arrangement is a big deal when you go to these exhibitor conventions. The people on the dais are trotted out to impress the audience, which is filled with theater owners. So they're invariably movie stars and important filmmakers. The purpose of these conventions is to sell movies to theater owners, to excite them. Senior executives and filmmakers sit on the dais and the exhibitors and junior executive-wannabes don't.

It was crucial for me to be seen on the dais. I wanted to be respected by filmmakers, and why should they respect me if they saw that my superiors did not treat me with respect?

A wannabe I was not. This was right before *Flashdance* came out, just before I was made senior vice president. *Footloose* was shooting. I was working with "talent" (the creative people), generating projects, getting attention. "How could Frank do this to me!" I wailed to no avail. I begged. I pleaded. Frank still wouldn't let me sit on the dais.

I couldn't believe it. "I'm not going!" I announced to Mancuso. But in his embracing, paternal manner, he talked me into it. I hated myself for going.

Paramount chartered a private jet and everybody was on the plane. Diller, Eisner, Simpson, Katzenberg. But also Steven Spielberg and Harrison Ford, who were about to embark on *Indiana Jones;* Jack Nicholson and Debra Winger, who were starring in *Terms of Endearment;* Eddie Murphy and Dan Aykroyd, who were in *Trading Places;* the *Airplane II* group; and John Travolta and Sylvester Stallone, who respectively were starring in and directing *Staying Alive,* the sequel to the highly successful *Saturday Night Fever.*

I was sulking in my seat when Frank Marshall, who was Spielberg's producer, said, "Dawn, do you know Martin Scorsese?" Oh. I do now. Thanks, Frank.

We clicked right away. I don't know what he was thinking of at the time, but what I was thinking was: THIS IS MARTIN SCORSESE!

He was already mythic to me. He'd already done *Mean Streets, Taxi Driver, Alice Doesn't Live Here Anymore, New York, New York* and my favorite, the flawless *Raging Bull*. He was about to direct *The Last Temptation of Christ*. He managed—just—to do things his way, which made him an outlaw. And I loved outlaws.

Fate made me pay for my good fortune, though. When we got to ShoWest, we went to a cocktail party before the big dinner. "Okay. Everybody on the dais, follow me," the executive running the event said. I was standing with Marty thinking, "What do I do now?" They started walking out, and Steven Spielberg turned around and called out, really loud, "Dawn, aren't you sitting with us on the dais?" No, Steven. Not tonight.

I trudged out and sat down at my table. I was pissed. I was embarrassed. But I was on air—I had just met Martin Scorsese. I looked at the dais, I couldn't take my eyes off of him. I was watching him in slow motion. He sat there for about ten minutes. Suddenly, he got up and snuck out. Why did he get up? Where was he going?! After our brief encounter, I already felt possessive.

A moment later, he was standing at my table. "Want to have a drink?" he said.

With all the cool I could muster, I leaped out of my chair.

We went gambling and we were pretty much inseparable from that moment on. When we came back from Las Vegas, we drove up the California coast and went from one romantic place to another. We fell in love. He was sexy and brilliant and funny and I was crazy about him.

I had moved to an apartment on Sunset Plaza when I was working on *Flashdance* and Marty moved out to L.A. from New York and moved in with me. A big deal for this die-hard entrenched New Yorker who hated to fly.

Our place was in a spectacularly beautiful art moderne 1930s building, with curved walls and moldings, and terraces with sensational views of the city.

I adored Marty. It was the first time I actually wanted to take care of someone and it was the first time someone would let me. He loved to stay up all night, watch movies, tape them and show me what was great about them. Which was terrific, except I had a day job. I couldn't afford to stay up all night. But I did.

There was an Orson Welles movie called *Touch of Evil* that Marty made me watch over and over again. He pointed out the opening shot, which was one single camera move, without cuts, that was legendary. Marty's excitement in watching it was inexhaustible, and I bet you he learned something different from it each time he watched it.

He had an extraordinary tape library. Marty had really been doing this all his life. As a child, he'd been ill with asthma. Movies had been his greatest pleasure and escape, and that was still true when he became an adult. When we lived together he still suffered from asthma. Stress would disable him. Smog would disable him. Cigarette smoke would cripple him. I would hear Marty downstairs at three o'clock in the morning, wheezing, hacking, barely able to breathe. I'd run downstairs and cradle him in my arms until his breathing returned to a regular rhythm.

Or he'd be taping some weird movie that no one had ever heard of but from which he remembered some scene, some camera move or an actor's moment. He'd nudge me in the middle of the night and say, "Look at this scene. Look at this scene!" He'd tell me why.

It was lucky for me. Watching classic films with Marty was an education. I started to look at how films were directed. I became conscious of things I never noticed before. How a camera move changes the scene, or how different lenses affect the moment, or what touches a director uses to embellish a scene.

After a bit, Marty went to a healer and his asthma subsided for the duration of our relationship. Of course, I always thought it was love that did it. . . .

But, aside from my classic film education, two good things came out of Marty's asthma, for me. One was that, after seventeen years, I stopped smoking. The other was *The Accused*.

One night, after one of his bouts, I lay mesmerized by a report on CNN about five men in New Bedford, Massachusetts, who had gang-raped a woman in a bar on a pool table. I watched this news story over and over and over again.

I said to Marty, "The thing I find so awful about this is that the people who witnessed and cheered the rapists on—the people who stood around and did nothing, didn't stop it, didn't call the police—were as guilty as the people who actually did the raping." I was outraged.

"Make it a movie," said Marty.

"What are you talking about?" I said.

"Make it a movie, Dawn," he said.

And I did. *The Accused* is the only movie I worked on in my Paramount days that felt completely like "mine," because it had been my idea from the beginning. In my mind, *Flashdance* had been about me.

This was about responsibility and moral courage. This was my protest march.

I pitched it. I had to beg because, on the face of it, it wasn't the most commercial idea I had ever pitched. But I got it into development and got a good first draft from Tom Topor, an ex–*Daily News* reporter who had written a play called *Nuts,* which was eventually turned into a movie by Barbra Streisand. Jeffrey asked me to assign the project to two producers on the lot, Sherry Lansing and Stanley Jaffe, with whom I was already working on *Fatal Attraction.* Stanley and Sherry had worked together successfully on *Kramer vs. Kramer,* she as its studio executive, he as its acclaimed producer. Stanley was also the youngest man since Irving Thalberg to have run a motion picture studio. He was president when he was barely thirty years old. Fortunately for me, they were two very strong allies: the movie would never have gotten made without them.

We continued to develop the script but it wasn't made into a movie until the next administration was running Paramount. Even then, I had a lot of trouble convincing the new studio chief, Ned Tanen, that we should make the movie. I was coming off *Top Gun* and the studio was feeling flush, so almost as a bone they threw me *The Accused.*

It was released in 1988, and Jodie Foster played the victim and won an Academy Award for her extraordinary performance. I remember her acceptance speech: "I'd like to thank my mother, who thought all my drawings were Picassos."

* * *

The fact is that my relationship with Marty changed my entire outlook towards movies and the creative process. Aside from anything else, his friends were artists, and unlike most studio executives, who only see one aspect of filmmaking, I now got to spend time with some of the best, most gifted directors in the business, people like Brian De Palma and Steven Spielberg. We went to dinner with George Lucas. Francis Ford Coppola made pasta for us.

Hanging out with Marty and his friends not only gave me an understanding and a relationship with creative people that would forever alter the way I thought about the business of making movies, but it also put me in the creative camp, unlike many other executives. I saw the creative people's side. I saw why they hated studio executives, why they always felt in an adversarial position with the studio.

Marty loved to call people like me "You-people," a noun that he pronounced Youpeople. Youpeople were the studio executives he thought were always trying to frustrate the process: the enemy. He would sputter, for example, "Youpeople have no idea what you're doing! Youpeople have never made movies!" I was to find out later that he was kind of right. But I didn't want to be a Youpeople. Early on, I got on the administrative track, but I tried to be as creative as I could within those limits. This was the beginning of my increasing unhappiness about being an executive.

One day, Marty introduced me to his friend, Gabriella Forte, who runs the Armani businesses worldwide. Knowing Gabriella had another kind of influence on me. She was a consummate, powerful, competent, feminine businesswoman. And she was shorter than I.

I got to know her well when Armani agreed to design some of the costumes for *The Untouchables*. Watching her operate reinforced the vitally important lesson I continually rediscover: It's only about the work.

When you walk into a room or into a meeting and all you're thinking about is whether you're going to say something smart, whether you're going to wow them, you're going to make mistakes. Because you're focused on you, you're not listening—you will miss things. They are not thinking about you. They're thinking about what needs to be done and looking for answers. When Marty is making a movie, he thinks only about the work. When Gabriella walks into a meeting, she is thinking only about the work.

She became a really important person in my life, and it was fascinating to see what she accomplished. Of course, Giorgio Armani is a genius and his designs are what people buy, but Gabriella is the one who carries out his vision. She was the first high-powered, highly successful female executive I knew intimately outside the movie business and her energy, style and guts made a big impression on me.

I began to wear Armani, but there were still problems, exemplified by my wearing these four-inch high heels all the time. Armani said that it takes a secure woman to wear flats. I knew that, but I just wasn't up to it.

But I'd come a long way, just to be able to withstand —and even enjoy—the publicity I started to get as Marty's girlfriend. It was with Marty that I first became a gossip column item and an object of interest to the paparazzi. Then, when *Flashdance* came out, I was the paparazzi's flavor of the month.

Six weeks after its release, we flew to Cannes because Marty's picture *The King of Comedy* was opening the festival that year. We stayed at the Hotel du Cap. I had never seen anything like this before. It was old-world elegant, full of antiques; I was convinced that Napoleon had sat in one of our arm chairs. What it actually was, I don't know, but it felt like three staff for every guest. Plus, I had never seen the Mediterranean before. I was happy to stay in my room and stare at the turquoise sea.

On opening night, while Marty was at his press conference, the limousine picked me up first. The Cannes Film Festival brought together celebrities from all over the world. And the narrow French streets were packed with tourists looking for their favorite stars. We picked up Marty and Robert De Niro at the Carlton Hotel and drove to the old Palais. They were very nervous. They knew what to expect. I had no idea. All I knew was I was sitting in the back of a French limousine, peering out my window at the exquisite Cannes, squished between Marty and Bobby De Niro, while behind us rode Sandra Bernhard and Jerry Lewis. The French love Jerry Lewis.

At the Palais, we got out of the limousine and before we could take a step, we were surrounded by the international press corps. They swooped down on us, enclosing us on all sides. For a moment, I was blinded by the incessant flash bulbs and the crush of human bodies. I felt like Tippi Hedren in *The Birds*.

Behind us, Jerry Lewis and Sandra were experiencing the same thing. But somehow, we inched toward each other so that we were now a group of five. We started slowly up the stairs. Marty took my hand and said, "I've got you," which was a good thing since I couldn't see one foot in front of me. Or behind me. Or to either side of me. It was a feeding frenzy; the photographers were in front of us, walking up the stairs backwards; they trailed inches behind us too, clicking and fluttering all around. You could hear the *whirr-whirr-whirr* of the motorized flashes, the screams of "Marty!" "Jerry!" "Bobby!" "Marty!" "Jerry!" "Bobby!" I was claustrophobic; there was no room to move except directly into this sea of black-tied paparazzi.

We got very little sleep that night. And the following morning, Marty and I left for Tunisia. It was to be half vacation and half a movie location scout for *The Last Temptation of Christ*.

We roamed the Sahara. We saw Bedouins, camel trains, stone structures that were built into the sides of mountains where Christ and his disciples may have stayed.

In Cannes, I felt like Tippi Hedren; now I was feeling like Lawrence of Arabia. I was in a state of wonderment and culture shock.

Marty and I loved being in the desert. We were happy there. There were no lights, no cameras, no phones.

I have a snapshot from that trip. Marty and I are perched perilously on the hump of a camel. The hapless camel, which had unbelievably bad breath and a flatulence problem, is on its knees. Its head is down, its hump is up; we're laughing so hard, it's all we can do to stay on.

My relationship with Marty lasted about a year and

it was the first time I had had a relationship that long with someone who wasn't married. It was truly a beginning for me.

The falling apart began as Marty got deeper into *The Last Temptation*. It was a very controversial movie and the attacks began almost immediately from people who thought he was blasphemous.

We'd been really happy together and I had become part of his family. I loved his parents and his daughters and for a while everything just seemed golden, but when the descent came, it was quick and brutal. As the movie neared production, the attacks on Marty by the religious right intensified and there were death threats.

We started to fight. I began to feel more and more excluded from his creative life. He had an assistant. I hated her. She didn't do anything to me but I hated her because it was her job to protect him and to wall him off and it's clearly what he wanted. So she started to interfere, getting between us, to protect him from anything outside.

It's hard to understand a director's obsession. You have to be one-dimensional when you're making a movie because it's so hard to get your vision onto the screen and so easy to lose it. You have to shut out everything. My experience is that most directors descend into an absorption with their movie that is complete, to the exclusion of almost everything else. And, typically, that means personal relationships.

Everyone wanted to take care of Marty, because he was very vulnerable. He attracted it, he loved it. And why shouldn't he love it?

I loved him still, in a way more and more, but as he got more depressed, a real nightmare began for me.

Marty was, like my father, loving and affectionate but, like my father, he had become closed emotionally to me. And like my father, Marty's passion was all dark, which made it both familiar, comfortable and painful. It was a replay of my childhood: the man who had made me so happy now had gone, before my eyes, to a dark place where I could no longer reach him.

Oddly enough, this awakened in me the realization of how much I needed to be cherished. My experience with Tom Hedley had made me clear-eyed enough so that I knew I could not stay in a relationship in which I would be brought down so low that it would be impossible to get back up. I knew that it was another kind of a man I should be with. Marty seemed to be that other kind of man. But it was not my time to be with him. To this day, Marty says it was around this time that the worst period of his life began.

I felt like I was drowning. From the outside, the pressures kept building. Many people wanted to use me to get to Marty. Including my bosses.

My life still somehow looked great, glamorous, enviable. Lynda, now a good friend, has told me that during that period she felt terribly jealous of me. She'd gone back to produce for David Geffen but felt invisible, isolated from *Flashdance*'s success, while I was having lunch with Ray Stark and dinner with Richard Pryor. Marty was the last straw. "When you moved in with Marty Scorsese I thought I was going to have a nervous breakdown," she told me later. "I thought of becoming a Buddhist monk."

Well, if she'd only known how dark it was in our home. In a way, it made me feel even more fraudulent that everyone thought my life was so enviable. But it couldn't go on much longer.

On Thanksgiving morning—around the time I was made senior vice-president of production at Paramount—Barry Diller called Marty at my apartment and said he wanted to see him at eleven o'clock in his office. When Marty got there, he was told Paramount had pulled the plug. The financing for *The Last Temptation* was being withdrawn. The protests had become too dangerous and the movie deemed too high a financial risk at Paramount. The religious right had triumphed.

Shortly afterward, *The Hollywood Reporter* ran a story saying *The Last Temptation* was officially canceled at Paramount. Adding to the humiliation for Marty, they reported it had been turned down by every other studio. It would be years before Marty was able to get that movie made. It was finally released in 1988.

Marty couldn't get over it. I'm sure he blamed some of it on me. Not directly, since I certainly had had nothing to do with the decision, hadn't even known about it. But he associated me with the Paramount management and I now personified the studio. I was a Youpeople. That was the beginning of the end.

Our relationship couldn't survive it. It didn't. Marty moved back to New York.

I went back to the south of France, but this time in mourning. I hid in a private hotel in St. Paul de Vence, sat by myself and sobbed. I was heartbroken.

One sleepless night, I phoned my friend Katherine in L.A. "What am I meant to learn from this?" I wept. "Just tell me. What am I meant to learn?" She said, "Maybe you finally learned what you don't want in a relationship. Now it's time to learn what you do want."

Here I was ready to kill myself, when a Michael Eisner postcard found its way to me. It was a postcard from his son's camp in Vermont. "Dear Dawn, I thought you'd like seeing my camp." I remember staring at the card and thinking: Michael has his priorities straight. He had his family life and his career in harmony and balance.

My life was a mess. My career was soaring but I was losing friends because I didn't have time to see them, and now I'd lost Marty. It's not easy to keep your equilibrium in these jobs. I admired Michael for his. He'd always leave a big meeting in time to get to his son's baseball game. He always made time for his personal life. I didn't.

After the breakup with Marty, I became totally preoccupied with work. I didn't date for a year. I guess it was my way of licking my wounds and it worked very well for me. Finally, though, my friends began to feel that the mourning was really going on too long. Marilyn Vance, a costume designer *(Pretty Woman)* who had become a very close friend, spent a lot of time talking to me about this. Or should I say listening to me talk about this, and talk about this, and talk about this.

She suggested I visualize. Like me, Marilyn had had some experience in visualizing, and she kept reminding me to see myself happy. I did, it worked, and now, whenever a friend is stuck and depressed I tell them the same thing. *It doesn't always work the first time, but if you insist on seeing yourself in a better situation or in a happier place, it helps get you back on track.* I can't always get myself to do it—sometimes I want to wallow. But when I actually do it, it invariably works.

I'll always remember how Marilyn looked at me,

very intensely, as if to will me back to normal, and said, *"Just let it go, Dawn.* Let it go."

And I did.

Luckily, work was going well. *Footloose,* released in February 1984, took in $8.5 million the first weekend, and was looking like nearly as big a hit as *Flashdance.* My first two movies—the ones that matter—were back-to-back hits.

Now I made some changes in my personal life. I allowed myself to become closer to my old friends. I had some new friends, too: Gabriella, with whom I had stayed friends after the breakup, and Nora Ephron, who had written *Heartburn,* which was being made into a movie at Paramount at the time, and whose extraordinary wit offered the invaluable luxury of many great laughs.

A couple of months after *Footloose,* Lynda called me. She said, "You did really great on *Footloose.* I've spent the last year feeling you cheated me of credit for *Flashdance.* But I didn't make *Footloose.* You made it."

I was overwhelmed that she would tell me this. I was tremendously moved. I remember tearing up as I asked her, "Would you be my date for the Women in Film lunch?"

"You bet, babe," said Lynda.

The Crystal Awards lunch was June 6, 1984. This was a big deal for women in the film business. We sat at the Paramount table. I may have been senior vice president of production, but in the Paramount hierarchy I was still a piker. We were at a table so far from the stage we were nearly in the kitchen. At least our food was hot.

It was the day Lynda and I really came to an

understanding. We went over what had happened and I said, "I should have been more understanding and generous, not so threatened. I should have tried to protect you more."

"You had to become a player," said Lynda. "If anybody could have fought for me then it was not going to be someone making her first movie. Then you started to soar. And when you start soaring, you can't carry everybody with you."

We watched Barbra Streisand get her Crystal Award, the highest honor from, and for, women in films. Barbra, one of my heroines, was becoming my friend. She made an amazing speech about the need for women to help other women. She told us how women had been hardest on her of all critics. (This is the very speech about which her mother had declared, "What's not to like?")

Lynda and I, however, were tremendously inspired. We started plotting together. I felt that day, as I have since, that Lynda became a friend and ally, instead of a rival in the jungle. Sitting in the pit, we put destructive competitiveness behind us and forged the kind of alliance women in Hollywood didn't have. We had not been high-powered allies doing deals and building a team like Michael Eisner and Jeffrey Katzenberg. We were too busy scraping each other up off the floor. Women then didn't have the experience of winning together; they only had the experience of losing as individuals. Boys learned these things from team sports and the locker room. Girls didn't, at least not then.

Men may sometimes feel threatened and competitive with one another, but they know a team can't win unless they work together. Some women in the movie business don't know this. I call it the locker-room syndrome. Locker rooms create a camaraderie among men. I was trained as a competitive swimmer so I knew it.

Moved by Barbra's speech, the hot food, and the renewal of our friendship, I suddenly exploded into optimism. After the speech, I said to Lynda, "I want a child. I want a family. I want a husband. I want to be head of production at Paramount within a year. And . . . I want the Crystal Award."

Lynda almost choked. "You've got a long way to go, bud," she said to me. "You haven't had a date in a year." And where, she asked me, did I think the head of production Jeffrey Katzenberg was going so I could have his job?

But all that mattered was that I'd been able to articulate and visualize my ambitions, even if they sounded grandiose and foolish.

And even if they sounded grandiose and foolish, now I was going to have to put up or shut up.

12

IT'S
ABOUT FUCKING
TIME

1984. WALTER MONDALE CHOOSES A WOMAN AS VICE-presidential candidate and Geraldine Ferraro becomes the first American woman to run for national office. She loses. Nude pictures are published of Vanessa Williams, the first black Miss America, and she returns the crown. Androgyny is a hit: Prince, David Bowie, Michael Jackson and Boy George clean up. The top songs are Prince's "When Doves Cry," Tina Turner's "What's Love Got to Do with It," Culture Club's "Karma Chameleon" and Madonna's "Like a Virgin." The big movies are *Ghostbusters*, *Indiana Jones and the Temple of Doom*, *Beverly Hills Cop*, *Gremlins* and *The Karate Kid*.

That winter, I went to Aspen with some friends. I was just learning how to ski. I loved it. As I rode up on the chairlift, my first time without an instructor, I noticed the guy on the seat next to me and he looked pretty cute. We started to talk. He asked me what I did for a living. Stupidly, I told him. And before we'd gotten to the top, he'd actually pitched me a story idea for a movie. I was in such a hurry to escape him that when I got off the chairlift, I tripped on my skis and fell flat on my face.

I was having trouble dating. No one was asking me out. If I wondered why, the answer was made crystal clear for me by an anecdote from my friend Craig Baumgarten.

Craig had been living with a woman who had stayed home for most of their relationship to take care of the house and him, something he'd gotten quite accustomed to. One day this woman decided to go to work. She was bored.

She started working really long hours. She was enjoying herself. It looked like it could be a career for her, not just a job.

But Craig was not happy. One night, having arrived home to an empty house several hours before she returned, he exploded. "If I wanted to live with a Dawn Steel, I would have lived with a Dawn Steel!"

I understood. But there was nothing I could do but wait for a man who wanted to live with a Dawn Steel.

So it was a big deal for me when I was asked out by Ned Tanen. He was president of Universal Pictures at the time. He was single. He was powerful. He was attractive and I had been watching him for months. In fact, he was very, as my mother would say, eligible. We met at a party and a couple of days later he asked me out to dinner.

That day, I had some minor surgery, resulting in a

dozen stitches on my upper thigh. Perhaps I should have canceled dinner with Ned, but I was really looking forward to it.

We went out to dinner at Morton's, which was and is the bastion of Hollywood power brokers. We had a really nice dinner and the scene at Morton's was fun and I was having a ball. I was actually having a date!

I left the table to go to the ladies' room. Then I looked down and saw that I was standing in a puddle of blood. I couldn't believe it. I had blood all over me. Was this really happening?

Yes. This guy had finally asked me out . . . and God was punishing me. For what?

I cleaned it up as best I could. I went back to the table and said to Ned, "I don't know how to tell you this, but I had a little surgery today and my stitches opened up."

So he took me to the hospital. Some date, right?

The next day Peter Morton of Morton's called Ned and said, "How does your date feel? Is she all right?"

Tanen said, "Why?"

"Because the man who sat in her seat after you left," said Morton, "looked down, saw blood on the seat, thought it was his blood, fainted and had to be taken away in an ambulance."

Ned and I went out a few more times but, clearly, there wasn't a romance in the cards for us.

I was heartened to hear that even Barbra Streisand dated schmucks. When I was senior vice president of production, Barbra called me one day. She'd heard about me and asked me to lunch to talk about whether

I'd be willing to run her production company. I went to the lunch though I didn't want the job: I wanted to go farther in a big studio first. But I wanted to know her. We became friends. We didn't talk business, we talked boys. I couldn't believe some of the guys she was dating. "You dated him?!" As if I were one to talk.

The hidden blessing was that I continued to develop relationships with women, often finding their company more interesting than men's, although it wasn't until later that the full meaning of this would become clear to me. Gradually, I was building trusting friendships. With my women friends I'd take trips, go bike riding, schmooze, have dinner, shop.

I also learned to enjoy my own company more and how to nourish myself. I strongly suggest that you *do something nice for yourself once a week*. It could be a facial or a good dinner out or shopping.

When things got really bad, though, I'd make a pilgrimage to the local Safeway. The word binge didn't begin to describe what I did. But the check out guy described it perfectly when he looked at the things that I'd bought—the salami, the Mallomars, the Mystic Mints, the Famous Amos chocolate chip cookies and the Eskimo Pies—and said: "Bad day, huh?"

Meanwhile, I kept working like crazy, just working. Paramount replaced family, husband, dog, everything. There was no time anyway. I went wherever I had to go to get done whatever had to be done. I was constantly traveling, always working.

In September of 1984, I was on location in Spain overseeing production on *Rustlers' Rhapsody*. (Okay, so I had a couple of bombs. It doesn't mean it was a bad movie.) My secretary tracked me down in the dusty outpost of Amería to say: "Mr. Diller is having a party Friday night for the twenty top Paramount people and Martin Davis. Mr. Diller wants you to be there."

This was on a Wednesday. I said, "Wait a minute, did you tell him I'm on location in Spain?"

"Yes, he wants you to be there."

I said, "Please call back and make sure you explain to him I'm on location in Spain."

The secretary called back and said, "He wants you there."

So I flew back. I didn't question it. If Barry Diller wanted me to come back from Spain to go to a party, I went.

When I arrived, he was standing at the entrance. He kissed me on the cheek and said, "I'm so glad you're here." Of course, I didn't know he said that to everybody else, I thought he said that only to me. I didn't know then that greeting each guest personally at the door, and expressing delight at each one's arrival, was part of Diller's totally charming way.

There were only three other women there—Helene Hahn, Susan Pile and Cecilia Andrews—and it was definitely just the top executives of Paramount and Gulf & Western. I still couldn't understand why I'd been asked to fly back, but I did my job and milled my way around the party. What was going on? Nobody knew and nobody asked.

The next day, September 12, 1984, there were banner headlines in *Variety:* Barry Diller had resigned from Paramount and was going to run Fox.

And that started the exodus. On September 22, Eisner was named CEO of Walt Disney. On October 1, Jeffrey Katzenberg was appointed president of motion pictures and television operations at the Disney studios. It was breathtaking.

Not only did it change my career profoundly, but it changed Hollywood profoundly. Diller would eventually create the fourth network, the Fox Broadcasting Company. Michael and Jeffrey would turn Disney, the sleeping giant, into a global empire. The Japanese began to pay attention to Hollywood. Things were never the same.

Paramount now entered a very strange transition period in which the slew of machinations, plotting, maneuvering and intrigues that surround every change of administration in a major motion picture studio took their course.

Let me cut to the chase. Because of the power vacuum left by The Departures, I was the senior ranking production executive and in this new capacity I had many new responsibilities. I was asked to host a screening of Stanley Jaffe and Sherry Lansing's *Firstborn*. The screening was at the Writers' Guild building on Sunset.

There I was, working the room, trying to make people feel comfortable, when Laurie Perlman, a C.A.A. agent, tapped me on the shoulder and said: "Dawn . . . do you know Chuck Roven?"

Now, I whipped around because I'd been hearing about Chuck Roven for a long time. The words seemed to fall out of my mouth. And with the profundity of Stanley greeting Livingstone, I said, "Well . . . It's about fucking time."

Unbeknownst to me, he'd been hearing about me, too. I guess a number of our mutual friends must have seen the possibilities. Marilyn Vance for one, was always chewing my ear off about Chuck. He had come into the movie business recently after a career as a successful arbitrageur. He was a producer who by then had a very fine film to his credit, *Heart Like a Wheel*. He was just coming into his movie career full-time, but somehow, we'd never run into each other before.

When I said "It's about fucking time," Chuck laughed. I liked that about him.

On our first date, I told Chuck I had a script of his on my desk and I was passing on it. The truth is, I hadn't read it, there hadn't been time, but I had to get this out of the way. I didn't want to be concerned that his script was the reason he wanted to be with me. I already knew that I was very attracted to Chuck. It didn't seem to bother him that I passed on his script. He seemed amused, if anything, by my directness. What a relief!

The lesson is: *Don't assume all men avoid strong women*. And, besides, we play a role here too. It's not just men who are uncomfortable with an untraditional balance of power. Often it's women, particularly if they are still looking for a man to take care of them. And the more successful you are, the harder it is to find.

And that doesn't even include all the women who are so burned out from trying to fill male role models that they don't even have the emotional wherewithal left to yearn for a romance, or to stay open to a relationship.

My iconoclastic opening line was not the only unusual element of our early relationship. When the doorbell rang at the time of our first date, I was watching an Herbalife convention on cable television. I, who always struggled with an extra ten pounds, was mesmerized by the testimonials of people who had lost hundreds upon hundreds of pounds by taking this Herbalife concoction.

Chuck either shared my curiosity or was entertained by it. We jumped in the car and drove to the Herbalife convention in Santa Monica. We spent our first date listening to Herbalife testimonials.

The next day, a lifetime supply of Herbalife arrived at my office. Chuck was irresistible.

Then I almost blew it. On our second date we went to a charity benefit, an industry event. Maybe I had forgotten how to date. I was preoccupied with who knows what. I acted badly. We had a fight. Chuck took me home. He didn't call again.

I remember saying to my shrink, "You know that Chuck Roven I told you about?"

"Yes?" Dee would say.

"He hasn't called me back. He's not for me, but maybe I should call him."

Then the next week, same office, same shrink, I said: "That Chuck Roven isn't for me, but maybe I should call him."

She said to me: "It seems to me like the first appropriate man you've talked about in a really long time. Maybe you should call *him.*" Right, maybe I should call him.

I still hoped he would call. I waited and waited and, finally, I called him.

"I'm glad you called me," he said.

"Would you have called me if I hadn't called you?" I asked him.

"No," he said. "You never would have forgiven me."

That was the moment I knew he was going to be my husband.

Katherine saw us a few months later. She said to me, "Dawn, you're wearing flat shoes. I know this must be the right man."

And Chuck is six feet tall.

Not only that, but she noticed that we laughed a lot. Like all the time. We did. We made each other laugh.

Chuck is my soul-mate. He made me feel like I was home. For the first time in my life, I was glad to be home. It was also the first time in my life I could visualize being a family with someone.

One night in an Italian restaurant with red and white checked tablecloths, Chuck proposed to me. On bended knee. He was partially hidden by the red and white checked tablecloth so I couldn't see he was on his knee.

"What are you doing down there, babe?" I said.

"I'm proposing!" he said.

We were ready to be married.

The main obstacle was Chuck's mother, Blanca. A

powerful Haute Jewish woman who had escaped from the Nazis, Blanca was a formidable prospect as a mother-in-law. We got off to a shaky start because at the time I was still estranged from my parents, and Blanca, surprised by my lack of evidence of a family, somehow got it into her head that, of all things, I was not Jewish. She was convinced I was pretending, to catch her son. I was enraged. "Who would pretend to be Jewish?! Six million people have been annihilated for being Jewish. Why would I fake it?"

Blanca tracked down my family. I was really upset at the time but it did serve to facilitate my reconnecting to my family.

Eventually, I took Chuck to Florida to meet my parents, so that it became clear to everyone—including myself—that I did indeed have a family and a Jewish one at that.

There was only one more trial to go through. In the eyes of the Jewish religion, I wasn't legally divorced. I had to get a "get," a Jewish divorce decree.

After Ronnie had agreed to divorce me, the rabbi who had married us then issued a corroborating document. Blanca sent her rabbi to New York to pick up the document and bring it back to Los Angeles. I thought I was now divorced. I was wrong.

Chuck's uncle, Bernard Spiegel, whom I adore, took me to the big *macher* Los Angeles rabbi. In the big *macher*'s study, the rabbi said something to me in Hebrew. I didn't have a clue what he said. Bernard told me to put the document, the one that the original rabbi had issued to the traveling rabbi, under my left armpit. I was then told to turn around in a circle three times.

I looked at Bernard. "Help," I said.

But Bernard indicated with his hand that I better start rotating. So I did.

I remembered something that had been told to me several years before, that in Orthodoxy, one of the prayers the men say each and every morning is, "Thank God I'm not a woman." As I rotated for the third and final time, I wondered if this was what they meant.

I was officially divorced. I'll always be grateful to Blanca. Not only did she reconnect me to my family, and help me get divorced, she also prepared Chuck for me. He understands strong women. He respects them and likes them. I got lucky. Really, really lucky.

On May 30, 1985, Chuck and I were married at the Stephen S. Wise Temple in Los Angeles, and then flew off to feed the pigeons in St. Mark's Square.

Within a year, I'd met my challenge, all except getting the Crystal Award, which would take a couple more years. But I was married to a man I loved and, in April of 1985, just ten months after I told Lynda that I wanted to be president of production, I got the title.

But lest you think I got more than a second of satisfaction, and lest you think I had time to get arrogant, let me tell you that the day I found out I had gotten the job, I went to a party at the home of Lew Wasserman, the legendary chairman of Universal Pictures. It was a big political fund-raiser, the first time I had been invited to his home. I walked around his house a couple of times. I didn't know many people. They were all senior to me in their respective corporate hierarchies. I lasted fifteen minutes and then I left.

I walked out of the party. As I waited for the valet to

get my car, I saw the chairman of Warner Brothers, Bob Daly, coming towards me with his hand outstretched. This is it. I've penetrated the inner circle. He knows who I am, I thought, as I stuck out my hand.

He handed me his parking ticket and said, "It's a white Mercedes."

13

YOU CAN'T
TEACH A PIG
TO SING

1985. ROCK HUDSON DIES OF AIDS. QUINCY JONES PRO-
duces "We Are the World," to help feed millions
of starving people and Bob Geldof organizes the
"Live Aid" concert to help end the famine in Ethiopia.
The top songs are "Careless Whisper," by Wham!;
"Say You, Say Me," by Lionel Richie; and
"Separate Lives," by Phil Collins and Marilyn Martin.
The big movies are *Back to the Future*, *Rambo:
First Blood Part II*, *Rocky IV*, *The Color Purple*, and
Out of Africa. Madonna is quoted as saying, "I knew
'Like a Virgin' would appeal to teenagers with active
hormones."

When Ned Tanen took over as president of the
Motion Picture Division at Paramount, my first
thought was, Thank God I didn't sleep with him! We'd

had those few dates a couple of years before. We never had an affair, but we were friends. And he respected me, I thought. He took me out to lunch at Mr. Chow's shortly after he took over at Paramount. I was so relieved that it was Ned in the job. It could have been anyone. And gleefully, I spoke my mind. "Boy, am I glad I didn't sleep with you."

But the palsy-walsy tone was not what Tanen had in mind. During that lunch he made it clear that our friendly social relationship would have to change and that our relations would henceforth be a good deal more formal. In fact, I came away from the lunch feeling uneasy and also very disappointed. What I'd hoped he would say was, "You're the new head of production."

I knew I was in line for it. I was the senior production executive left at Paramount, once all the other Diller people had gone. I was the only link to the old administration, and as my friend Joel Silver said, "the only person who knows what the fuck is going on at this studio." I saw that as an advantage. Tanen didn't.

My record was great. I'd been tested. I wanted him to give me the title. I felt I'd earned it. But Ned made it clear that he would have to spend time watching me to see how I worked, and to see who else was available for the job. It was humiliating.

So we began in a much more suspicious, much more formal relationship than what I'd hoped. It turned out to be so damn formal, in fact, that for the entire time I worked for Ned Tanen, I had no idea what to do to salvage our ease. I couldn't understand him at all. I didn't know how to please him. I tried everything. I tried passion. I tried hard work. I tried flamboyant demonstrations of competence. I tried great instincts. I tried great contacts. I tried cajoling. I told him jokes. I tried everything and nothing worked. I could never tell where I stood with him, not ever. My confidence sank.

The fact was that I had to learn to play with a brand new team. It wasn't just Ned Tanen. When Diller left, instead of replacing him with Michael Eisner, Davis chose as chairman the more malleable Frank Mancuso, the guy Ned called "The Booker From Buffalo."

Under Barry Diller, Frank had risen to president of the motion picture division. Frank had a kind of Italian street aesthetic, big pointy collars on his shirts, a very soft-spoken way of speaking. People thought of him as a kind, paternalistic but powerful Godfather.

They were wrong.

Somehow—and this was the miracle—he managed to convince Martin Davis that he was a better man for the job than Michael Eisner, that he could run the entire studio: movies, TV, video, foreign, the whole enchilada.

The environment changed when the new top management came in with its new corporate and moviemaking ideology. Barry Diller and Michael Eisner had come from television. They believed in high-concept movies: if you have a clear idea at the core of a movie, an idea that you can describe in a sentence or two or three, you can still market a movie that's not great. The flip side of that is a movie like *Tender Mercies*. It's a really well-made movie with no clear idea at its core. And it was impossible to market. Consequently, very few people went to see it.

The high-concept idea was what Paramount was about during the late seventies and the early eighties, and it worked. It worked over and over and over again. We had a string of hits that other studios envied. Michael and Barry had a run that went on for almost ten years, an unheard-of accomplishment.

The new group was composed of older men who had a more traditional way of working. It wasn't about passion. It was about business.

Ned Tanen was brilliant but mercurial; a mysterious, dark and brooding boss. Though he was very good at his job and had a long and impressive track record, withholding approval was his management style. And by withholding approval, he made everyone who worked for him dance to get it.

To be fair, it has to be stated that Ned was miserable in the job. He hadn't truly wanted it and only took it to extricate himself from an even more painful political situation at Universal. By the time he got to Paramount, to say that he was ambivalent about his work was an understatement. He was always threatening to quit, and used it as leverage to refuse any corporate responsibilities. There wasn't much anyone could do to him. He had them by the balls because there was no one else available who could do the job.

There are legendary stories about his moods. And he could be really intimidating. For instance, it was well known that when people who were starting out would come and pitch to Ned, he had been heard to say: "I'm in the movie business. I make movies. You're not. Give me a reason to put you in the movie business."

Chuck tells an amazing story about him. When Ned was running Universal, Chuck and Michael Laughlin (his producing partner on this movie) were in his office trying to cast their movie. Chuck had optioned the rights to *Dick Tracy* in 1978.

The actor Chuck and his partner were desperate to get to play Dick Tracy was Warren Beatty. (And, of course, Warren Beatty went on to direct and star in *Dick Tracy*. Great minds think alike.) But when Warren Beatty's name was mentioned as someone interested in the project, Ned said, "This is nothing but a jerk-off. Warren never makes up his mind. It's never going to happen."

So Chuck and Michael were trying to convince him to let them go out and make a firm offer of sizable cash to Warren Beatty. Michael Laughlin had a relationship with Warren, they knew each other very well, so Chuck and Michael told Ned they would be able to get Warren to read it.

And Ned said, "No chance, he'll never read it, he takes forever to make up his mind."

And Laughlin said to him, "Ned, that's why filmmakers hate you, because you're so negative, you're always so negative. That's why filmmakers don't want to be here at Universal."

There was nothing on Ned's desk. He always had the cleanest desk, except a little white note pad and some No. 2 Everwrite pencils neatly lined up. As Michael was going into a tirade about how negative Ned was, Chuck could see that Ned was starting to fume. Smoke was starting to come out of his ears. Finally, he picked up a pencil and he said, "Okay, you got it."

He threw the pencil at Laughlin and it stuck in his chest. Tanen said, "You have forty-eight hours. If you don't have an answer from Warren Beatty in forty-eight hours, I'm canceling the project."

He made no comment about the pencil sticking in Michael's chest and neither did anyone else. He had this No. 2 Everwrite lead pencil sticking in there and now a little blood was starting to circle on his white shirt. But nobody said anything.

Laughlin finally said, "Okay, fine." He carefully removed the pencil from his chest, said to Ned, "You'll probably need this," and put it on his desk. He and Chuck then walked out. Forty-eight hours later they did not have an answer and the project was canceled.

So this was the guy I was working for, and this is what I had in mind all the time, the pencil sticking out of the chest. I was just waiting until it was sticking out of mine.

But I forgot about all of that the day I got the head of production job.

Ned had wanted Sean Daniel, an executive at Universal, or Bruce Berman, an executive at Warner Brothers. But neither of them was available. One day, five and a half months after Ned began his tenure, he called me into his office. "Congratulations," he said flatly. "It's yours." Good-bye, good luck, break a leg.

I was thrilled. I was only the third woman to have a chance at this job, preceded by Sherry Lansing at Fox and Paula Weinstein at United Artists.

To celebrate, Chuck took me to Las Vegas to see the Hagler/Hearns middleweight championship boxing match, traditionally an event frequented by the "Hollywood Studio Boys Club." And the boys were there.

I had never been to a fight before. It was the most violent exhibition I had ever seen. I hated it. We were sitting so close to the ring that blood splattered all over me. Perhaps I should have taken it as a sign.

But I was too excited about my new job. On April 16, 1985, the front page of *Variety* announced:

DAWN STEEL NEW PREZ OF PROD'N AT PAR

Some of the text went on to say:

Dawn Steel, the first woman elevated to a comparable executive post at a major studio since Sherry Lansing was president of Twentieth Century Fox Prods., is the new president of Production at Paramount Pictures . . . The job was vacated when Jeff Katzenberg resigned five and a half months ago to join Paramount President Michael Eisner at Walt Disney Prods . . .

. . . Steel's choice was anything but a fait accompli. Although she was a candidate from day one, she was considered a long-shot . . . Tanen called reports of Steel being first in-line premature and without merit . . . He said at the time that a number of production executives at the studio were viable possibilities . . .

Not exactly what you'd call a mandate. But nothing could ruin my enthusiasm. I put together my staff, a talented and eclectic group: Lindsay Doran, brilliant, whimsical and eccentric, who was ultimately responsible for the movie *Ghost;* David Madden, a writer's dream, who taught me more than I taught him about story and structure; and Michael Besman, who bounced from one great idea to another with all the excitement and abandon of a newborn colt. And I had inherited David Kirkpatrick from the former administration.

I promoted Michael Roberts, Teddy Zee and Lance Young to creative executives.

I loved my staff. But my honeymoon was short-lived.

Ned was spending a lot of time at his house at the beach. He seemed disinterested in us. He had been doing this job for twenty-seven years in one way or another and he was bored. When something came up when he was at the beach, he'd say to me, "Handle it. Just handle it." But then, he'd come back from the beach upset that decisions had been made without him.

Let's take, for example, *The Untouchables.* After the producer, Art Linson, and I hired David Mamet to write the screenplay, Ned announced he hated David Mamet's work. Art and I wanted Brian De Palma to direct the movie. Ned announced he was against De Palma. We wanted to make the movie starring Kevin

Costner. Ned insisted that Costner wasn't a movie star and forced us to surround him with "established" stars. We got Sean Connery. Connery wasn't enough for Ned either, so we then got De Niro to play Al Capone even though De Niro demanded two million dollars for ten days' work.

That process was a studio executive's nightmare. Yet, who's to say that he was wrong? The fact is that the movie worked. Big time. Ned was yin and I was yang, but maybe you needed both points of view.

It was a shame we didn't get along because there was a lot to learn from him. Ned's a really smart guy, his instincts are great, he's been in the business for a million years and he can see trouble coming down the pike a million miles away. When he wasn't angry he could be both charming and funny. A very attractive man, and very bright, but sardonic, unhappy and unreadable. I always knew where I stood with Barry and Michael and Don and Jeffrey. Not with Ned. Not ever.

People often wonder what it is that studio executives do. Once we get into production, mostly, we're backstops. We see problems that others have missed and try to solve them. These can range from big problems such as budgets or script problems to seemingly small dilemmas.

For instance, around this time I was working on *Top Gun,* Simpson and Bruckheimer's follow-up to *Flashdance,* and they had just delivered Tom Cruise for the starring role.

Here we had the most handsome guy in Hollywood to star in this $20 million movie and you couldn't see his face because he was in a pilot mask. Every time they went up in their planes—and they went up a lot—you couldn't tell who was who. In the end we cheated by putting their names on the helmets and dropping their face masks whenever we could.

We were also prepping *Fatal Attraction*. Ned, who didn't believe in this movie, refused to have anything to do with it. The filmmakers, Sherry and Stanley and Adrian Lyne and Michael Douglas, were searching for the female lead and they were having trouble.

Glenn Close, already an accomplished actress but not as visible as she was about to become, pleaded to read for this part. She came in with no makeup and she read for Adrian. He held the video camera himself. There was no lighting. Adrian was so excited about what he had gotten on tape that he picked up the tape and brought it across the lot to show it to me in my office. Glenn Close had transformed herself from an elegant thespian into a harpy. It was an extraordinary performance. The rest is cinema history.

During this time, I was also having trouble with *The Accused*. Ned didn't want to make the movie and he kept putting it off. It took the success of *Top Gun* for me to convince him to green-light *The Accused*. He finally agreed to let us go ahead, but only with a budget of under $7 million. He thought that would kill it, that we wouldn't be able to make it for that small a budget. But the $7 million figure didn't deter us. We were willing to make it under the most difficult circumstances. Ned had underestimated our commitment and passion to the project.

I was having trouble getting new movies made. It was hard for Ned to call off projects that were already in the green light lane. But I was having problems getting new scripts made into movies. One such project was *Good Morning, Vietnam,* which I loved and was desperate to make. Another was *Ghost.*

One man's turnaround is another man's hit. The irony was that *Flashdance* was Ned's turnaround and was my hit. *Good Morning, Vietnam* was about to be Ned's turnaround and Jeffrey Katzenberg's hit. When it became clear that I would not be able to get this movie made, Robin Williams and Larry Brezner, the coproducer and Robin's manager, came to me and asked me, as a personal favor, if I would put the movie in turnaround. Since I had failed for months and months to get it made, I sadly agreed.

I called Jeffrey Katzenberg and told him I was sending him a script. I told him I couldn't get it made and maybe he would want to make it.

More cinema history. But this time it belonged to another studio.

In the end, many of the movies I worked on were hits, so Ned wound up having to give me the head of production job after all. But the toll in insecurity and paranoia was incalculable, even when the movies did well! And even when I was officially named president of production, Ned was reluctant and acted very disenchanted with me. Before finally giving me the title, he let me know that he was thinking of and talking to other people, so that by the time I got it I was utterly humiliated.

* * *

Ned played other executives off of me so that I always felt unclear as to where my authority began and ended.

One particular guy who benefited from Ned's style was Kirkpatrick. He was a reader when I arrived at Paramount and had risen to the job of being Jeffrey Katzenberg's grunt, but it was Ned who really promoted him. He was now a senior executive.

There's a saying: *Never try to teach a pig to sing. You waste your time and you annoy the pig.*

Kirkpatrick, a bald, former Jesuit student, whose smile never looked real, had the dubious distinction of being the executive with the longest run without a hit. We used to have a pool: When will Kirkpatrick get a hit? It didn't happen during my tenure. In fact, he became known as "The Teflon Executive," because wherever he went, failure always followed. But for the longest time, it seemed that the bombs never stuck to him.

He was perfect for Ned. I would make a statement and Ned would let Kirkpatrick dump all over what I said. Ned would take Kirkpatrick's side and the cheese stands alone.

As Machiavellian as he was, Kirkpatrick rose to Ned's task with relish. And I started feeling that I was being not only gaslighted, but blowtorched.

Kirkpatrick must have thought the job was only about politics. I thought my job was only about the work. We were both wrong.

Then there was Frank Mancuso's son, Frank, Jr., quite a trendy, preening figure around the office, always wearing hip, unconstructed jackets with big shoulders and jeans. He was very handsome. He knew it. It looked like he shaved his eyebrows but he didn't pluck them below the surface so you could always see the stubble. Otherwise he was very carefully groomed.

Junior, a producer, hated me. I can't blame him, since I didn't want to green-light any of his movies. The level of his commercial taste was equal only to that of his friend Kirkpatrick.

But I made a big mistake. I should have co-opted him. I should have befriended him. He was the son of the chairman of the board. He was much more dangerous than I had ever imagined.

As I got more insecure, I got more difficult with my staff and with myself. I began to hate going to work. Sunday nights were horrible. In fact, Sunday nights were horrible for me as long as I was an executive at a major studio, right until I left Columbia Pictures. I never felt prepared for Monday mornings.

The workload was awesome and there was no time off, no evening to myself and my husband, no weekends. There were eleven or twelve and sometimes as many as twenty scripts that had to be read on a weekend. It was hard to get through all of them, and what I did read, I didn't remember.

It was scary to read all those scripts and not remember what I'd read. Luckily, I did remember how I felt. I always remembered the essence of the script, and whether I thought it was a good movie idea. But I couldn't remember individual scenes or how it ended or began. I was afraid I could never keep up this pace, I would never get all the work done.

Meanwhile, there was this growing brouhaha about my reputation and my success. Liz Smith wrote an article about me in *Vogue,* in which she called me "the most powerful woman in Hollywood," and others soon followed. But I surely didn't feel that way.

I once read an article in a business magazine in which successful CEOs were asked "What is your greatest fear?" And they all answered the same thing: "What am I going to do when they find out I'm not as good as they think I am?"

Lynda, Katherine and another friend, Rosalie Swedlin, gave me my wedding shower at Rosalie's house. Rosalie was the most senior female agent at C.A.A.

About thirty women came. At the time Lynda called it a power shower, and as far as we knew it was the first coinage of the term. What was great about it was that all the women there were women who had accomplished something in their own right.

Barbra Streisand caused quite a stir in the neighborhood by writing down the wrong address. She wandered this Bel Air street, ringing doorbell after doorbell, in a white pants suit and a white hat. Can you imagine opening your door to find Barbra Streisand standing alone on your doorstep inquiring, "Is this Dawn's shower?"

After lunch, a video tape was shown, narrated and

produced by Katherine and directed by Polly Platt. It was called *Men of Steel*. On the tape were interviews with a lot of the men in my life, ex-boyfriends, business associates, men friends, talking about their relationships with me. Barbra did "the score." Of all songs in the history of songs, the one I hated most was a misogynistic ditty called "To All the Girls I've Loved Before," sung by Willie Nelson and Julio Iglesias. Barbra, knowing how much I hated it, wrote and sang her own version of it. It went like this:

> To all the men who shared my life,
> Well, I'm now gonna be someone else's wife.
> But I'm glad they came along,
> And I dedicate this song,
> To all the men I've loved before.

A miracle happened. I got pregnant. Chuck and I were thrilled. We bought a beautiful and romantic house in Bel Air, an old pool house built in the thirties. The garden had been designed by Cecil Beaton. I loved it and it was the place I escaped into when work became increasingly hellish. I spent weekends, excitedly designing and redesigning the baby's room. I had waited a decade to get pregnant again and I was blissful. I was transported.

Physically, it was an easy pregnancy. I was never even nauseated. But I was exhausted and hormonal.

Dr. Margolin told me that I could tell people I was pregnant, once I'd had a sonogram and had heard the baby's heartbeat. He explained that once you hear the heartbeat, the chances of miscarriage are greatly diminished.

Chuck and I were in the examining room. I watched the little monitor while Dr. Margolin did the sonogram. Suddenly, I heard this soft but sure sound. A confident sound. And then I saw a tiny blip on the monitor. It was pulsing to the beat of the soft but sure sound. It was my baby's heartbeat. I had never heard music like that before.

I told Frank Mancuso that I was pregnant over breakfast and he said he was thrilled. I truly believed he was thrilled.

14

HONEY, YOU'RE HORMONAL

1986. SIMONE DE BEAUVOIR AND CARY GRANT DIE. ALL OF America watches, horrified, as the *Challenger* explodes on national TV. *Lonesome Dove* wins the Pulitzer prize. The top songs are "That's What Friends Are For," by Dionne Warwick and friends; "Walk Like an Egyptian," by The Bangles; and "On My Own," by Patti LaBelle and Michael McDonald. The big movies are *Top Gun, Crocodile Dundee, Platoon, The Karate Kid: Part II,* and *Star Trek IV: The Voyage Home.*

* * *

In Rome on my honeymoon, I had received a telegram:

Dear Dawn and Chuck: we wish you a lifetime of happiness. Congratulations, with love.
Frank and Faye Mancuso.

But somehow, everything changed with the pregnancy, with Frank Mancuso. Maybe it had changed beforehand and I wasn't aware of it. Maybe Ned had poisoned Frank's mind against me and I didn't know it. Maybe Frank had poisoned Ned to me and I didn't know it. Maybe I had poisoned them. But they didn't like me anymore. Period.

I was exhausted. I would have been exhausted anyway, not just from the work, but from meeting so many demands with so little support. Meanwhile, I was on the mood roller coaster of pregnancy. I was being pressured from above, and in my horrendous hormonal state I started pressuring below and became even more demanding of the people who worked for me than I had ever been.

Your secretaries and your assistants reflect you. They are the first aspects of your operation the outside world experiences. My fear was that an incompetent office was an absolute reflection of me. And it was.

It was around this time that I started to get a reputation for being difficult. That's when the real bad press started.

I'd been trained by the Diller–Eisner team to be loud and passionate and direct. I didn't realize for the longest time that I was intimidating. I didn't know that when I walked into a room that some people were already scared of me.

The truth is, I had a short fuse when I was threatened. Ned's constant criticism reminded me of my mother's criticism. I felt I could do no right. So in turn, I became hypercritical of myself and of those who worked for me.

It was not my proudest hour.

The world was becoming more and more menacing to me. Word got out that I was tough on my staff, and soon it was the buzz around the lot, and eventually that buzz made its way out beyond Paramount.

According to my friends, Ned's toadies were making sure the word was spread. For instance, I learned that Kirkpatrick, who ostensibly reported to me, was undermining me with my staff, telling them, "If you're having trouble with Dawn, if you can't talk to Dawn, come to me. Tell me about it." The press was beginning to pick it up. It started to snowball. Soon I had to read about myself in captions like "The Queen of Mean."

I had certainly made some mistakes dealing with Ned. I was too oppositional. Maybe I was too tough with Ned on the *Fatal Attraction* battle, too proprietary about the movie. Maybe I was too edgy. Maybe I was too frank. Probably I wasn't as respectful or sensitive to Ned as I could have been or should have been.

But sometimes you have to accept that there are bosses and colleagues whom you can never turn around. Instead of going home frustrated and torturing yourself and the people around you, move on and find another way. There are people with whom you pass a point of no return and you should give up on them.

That was definitely the case with Ned. I was at that point of no return.

* * *

As I got more pregnant, things got worse. It's really something being pregnant in a corporate setting, in any office, let alone a Hollywood corporation.

The first time my breasts met my stomach was a profound moment for me. They just lay there. Resting. Immovable. It was an amazing thing to me. And I had to buy a bra for the first time in my life.

And one of my favorite consolations was gone: I couldn't go shopping. The only thing I could buy was shoes. At the end, my feet were so swollen that I couldn't even do that.

I was depressed, and I was scared of childbirth, because of what my mother had been through and because I was forty years old. I was miserable about work, but excited about the baby, keeping an image of a happy baby in my head. It was a completely schizophrenic time for me.

I no longer walked, I waddled. I had to pee constantly, so in the middle of meetings, I'd push myself up and out of my chair, waddle out with my huge breasts leaning on my huge stomach. Then waddle back.

For the life of me, I could not figure out what to wear. I had seen other women look great pregnant. I was not one of them. My old clothes, the ones I'd relied on to give me dignity and presence in the world, no longer fit. It was hard to imagine that they ever had. Whatever I put on looked terrible.

Fortunately, Chuck was around. And we laughed a lot. We went to Lamaze classes with friends—Lucy Fisher, who's a senior executive at Warner's, and her husband, Doug Wick, producer of *Working Girl*.

Lamaze classes were about teaching you to breathe

through labor pains. There were different breaths for different phases of labor. Lucy and I were very good breathers. The same could not be said of Chuck and Doug, who were assigned the job of breathing with us. Inhale, exhale . . . Inhale, exhaleexhaleexhale. This cracked them up. Plus, every time I exhaled, I either peed or farted. This was not a dignified period of my life. But it was funny.

Lucy, who became a really good friend of mine during this time, was a highly respected studio executive. She had made a conscious decision not to go for a president of production job like I had. She'd decided she wanted to have several children and that was more important to her than advancing her career.

Sometimes, when I went to the office, I envied her her decision.

My moods swung like a swing. There were days I was on the verge of tears all the time. I just knew my enemies were plotting against me, but in my hormonal state it was really tough to separate paranoia from progesterone. I was moody but rational, and I did some of the best work of my career during this time.

I was beginning to have a vague sense of isolation. Things were happening without my knowledge. I was beginning to be excluded from meetings, meetings that I should have not only attended but led. I started to hear about deals being made that I knew nothing about, projects put into development that had never been discussed with me.

I went to Ned. I said, "What's happening? What's wrong? What am I doing wrong? You are clearly unhappy with me." Ned said, "Go away. There's nothing wrong." And then told me a bad joke.

Maybe I was being paranoid. I felt surrounded by people plotting against me. Probably because they were. Maybe the studio was just gearing itself up for when I would be gone during my maternity leave. What else could they do?

But the gossip intensified and the period right before my daughter was born was a terrible time. I was depressed and very angry. I was scared to death that all the negativity in my body was going to affect my baby.

But I was still doing my visualizations. Six months earlier, I had seen a beautiful baby standing up in a stroller. I had never seen a face like this, the happiest face I had ever seen in my life. It was an image that defined bliss itself for me, and for the duration of my pregnancy, I just focused on that baby.

At work, every once in a while there'd be a red herring that would make me think things were all right. In January, parent company chairman Martin Davis wrote me a letter of congratulations for doing such a great job, and thanked me for staying when he needed me.

In late February, just weeks before I was due, the March issue of *GQ* hit the stands with a story in which I was named as one of the "35 most important people in Hollywood." In the article on "Hollywood's Most Powerful" I was cartooned on the title page with Diller, Ovitz, Spielberg, Stallone, Cosby, Stark, Wasserman, etc. Frank Mancuso got a reference in the story. Ned Tanen, head of the studio, wasn't even mentioned.

Now I was in big trouble.

My publicity caused very mixed reactions at Paramount. Frank Mancuso said at the time, "Ned's jealous of your attention in the press."

I was given a baby shower, which was cohosted by Lynda and the Mancuso women: Faye Mancuso, Frank's wife; Maria Mancuso, their daughter and Frank, Jr.'s sister; and Becky Mancuso, Frank, Jr.'s wife at the time. I loved all three of these women. I still do.

I was very attached to Faye. To me, she was the storybook mother, the embodiment of unconditional love.

A lot of women I loved came. It was the first time I felt part of a sisterhood. I knew that some of the women were here because I was a production head and they had deals with the studio. But they were also all women I liked and admired, and they liked me. I felt like a member of a sorority of bright, energetic, remarkable women. It was like being a Kiltie all over again.

My mother and Blanca, my mother-in-law, gawked. There was Bette. There was Barbra Streisand, Diane Keaton, Carrie Fisher, Penny Marshall, Maria Shriver. There were writers, directors, agents, executives and producers. And they were all women.

I had a ball. I loved the food, I loved my guests, I loved unwrapping all the baby's presents. And she received so many special gifts that I didn't have to buy anything for Rebecca for three years.

That shower was a very important event for me. In a way, all my worlds came together that day, my masculine world of power and the new feminine world that I was discovering in myself with my marriage and my pregnancy. In fact, this was the beginning of resolving many of my problems regarding my mother, and, not coincidentally, the beginning of many rich, trusting and meaningful relationships with other women.

I felt everything was going to be all right the day the three Mancuso women gave me my shower.

15

IT'S ONLY BUSINESS

1987. IT'S IMPOSSIBLE TO TURN ON THE RADIO WITHOUT hearing a song from Michael Jackson's *Bad*.

They never tell you the truth: pregnancy does not last nine months. It lasts ten months. They count up to forty weeks until B-day. You figure it out, no matter how you compute it, it's not nine months.

I was in my tenth month. I could not find a comfortable position. I had gained thirty-five pounds but I hadn't gotten any taller. In order to lift my breasts into that bra, I needed a forklift, and I looked like a mutant pear.

My baby was due in several weeks. I had told Frank and Ned that I would stay home on maternity leave for a month. And then I'd enroll Rebecca in the Paramount Day Care Center, which had been started by Gary David Goldberg for his children and his *Family Ties* crew, and by Rhea Perlman for her children and those of the *Cheers* group.

It was a good day care center, and I loved the idea that Rebecca would be so close to me. I could take her with me in the morning, visit her during the day, stop by anytime I wanted, then pick her up and take her home with me.

I had it all figured out.

When my labor started at two A.M., I got out of bed and moved to my favorite chair. I didn't want to wake Chuck yet; I knew it would be hours before we had to go to the hospital. And I wanted to sit quietly and dream about my baby's arrival. I also wanted to finish the trashy gothic paperback novel which kept my mind off the labor pain.

Chuck woke up at his usual time, five A.M., and found me sitting in the chair watching the sun rise, inhaling and exhaling loudly. Inhale, exhale-exhaleexhale.

Calmly, we drove to the hospital, went to admitting, and checked in, breathing all the way. We were sent up to the labor rooms, where a resident examined me. "You're not ready yet," he said. "Come back in a couple hours."

It was a beautiful March morning. Chuck drove us to the La Brea Tar Pits, a tourist attraction in L.A., a prehistoric mudscape where dinosaurs supposedly got stuck, like in quicksand, and were buried. I had never been there before. Every time I had a bad contraction, Chuck held me while the dinosaurs looked on. He breathed with me. And he didn't laugh. I now understood the purpose of Lamaze; those contractions literally take your breath away.

I called Dr. Margolin several times from various phone booths. "Can't you give me anything for this pain?" I pleaded. He couldn't. He didn't want to slow down the contractions and there was apparently an additional risk involved in giving painkillers to women over forty.

Chuck drove me around for hours, trying to take my mind off the pain. He took me to a mall, but that only seemed to increase my contractions. Finally, I started to dilate and the hospital admitted me. It was two o'clock in the afternoon.

I will never forget that labor room. I had now been having serious contractions for about twelve hours. The sounds of women screaming in many different languages pierced the air. Pretty soon, they all blended into one screaming voice: AAAAaaahyeEEE!!!! AAAAaaahyeEEE!!!! All I could think was, Oh my God, what's happening to these women and is it going to happen to me?!

Yes it is. And it did.

There's no dignity in childbirth. There's joy, but no dignity. You've already heard about the bladder problems and the flatulence and the moment when there's no longer any space between your breasts and your stomach and the hormones and the forty-week-long endurance test. But you're still not prepared for the everything-hanging-out of it all. You get used to it really fast.

Suddenly, in mid-contraction, Dr. Margolin looked at the fetal monitor and calmly said, "We have a problem. The umbilical cord is wrapped around the baby's neck. She's not getting enough oxygen. Her heartbeat is irregular. We're going to have to get her out immediately."

After that everything happened really fast. I kept screaming, "Where's Chuck? Where's Chuck?" Poor Chuck had stepped out for one minute to go to the bathroom when this started.

"Please wait! Wait for Chuck," I cried as they wheeled me out of the labor room toward the emergency OR. "Don't do anything without Chuck!"

Remember in *Ben Casey* when the doors banged against the walls as the stretcher was thrust through the doorways? That's the way the gurney sped toward the operating room with me on it. Chuck was already there. And then I was in the operating room and there was this really nice anesthesiologist. He calmed me right down. He promised me that he'd make the pain go away. And then he asked me about *Flashdance*.

Then the painkiller, the epidural, started to work and Dr. Margolin started the C-section. There was a green cloth covering me from my waist down, and all I kept thinking was that Chuck was going to peek. I was desperate: "Promise me you won't look." He promised. And held my hand.

What seemed like seconds later, she was out. Dr. Margolin held her up for me to see. I was sobbing. He asked Chuck if he wanted to cut the umbilical cord. But Chuck was convinced that he would hurt me.

I was numb from my neck down so I couldn't hold the baby. Chuck held her. But from my neck up, I knew that this was the greatest moment of my life.

I had my child. We named her Rebecca Steel Roven.

It had been quite a night for the Steel family on both coasts. Rebecca had been born at eight o'clock at night. My brother Larry's son Jesse was born in New York hours earlier. My ecstatic mother, who had waited so long for one moment like this, now had two. She didn't know what to do first.

I had a belly full of stitches but I felt no pain. I was blissed out. At eight o'clock the following morning, I was in my little hospital room with Rebecca in my arms. She took to breast-feeding immediately, which is more than can be said for her mother.

Chuck was in a state of shock. Overnight, we had become a family. He had become a family man. He sat on the edge of the bed, staring at his baby and me. "She looks just like I did when I was born," said my husband.

"What are you talking about?" I laughed. "She doesn't look like anyone."

"Look at her. Just look at her. She has my nose, she has my lips . . ."

I looked at my child. She had nothing of the kind.

"The truth, Chuck, is that Rebecca looks more like Dean than you."

Dean Martin, Jr., was Chuck's best friend in the world. And he had become one of mine over the years. Dean was a golden boy, an actor, the most beautiful, funniest, heavenly son of Dean Martin. Everyone loved him.

Chuck looked at his daughter. "I can think of worse things," he said.

The phone rang. It was the first phone call we'd had. Chuck picked it up, said hello, listened, then handed the phone to me. "It's Ned."

With Rebecca in my arms, I put the phone to my ear. "Hello?"

"Congratulations," said Ned.

"Thank you," I said. There was a long, uncomfortable pause. And then I said, "Thanks for calling."

"Good-bye," said Ned. And he hung up.

I handed the phone back to Chuck. "Well, that was nice," I said.

"What'd he say?" asked Chuck.

"Not much. Just congratulations." I smiled. "He was our first congratulations call."

Several hours later, Chuck went down to the coffee shop for breakfast. When he returned, he looked sick.

"What's wrong, honey?" I asked. Rebecca was asleep in my arms.

"Nothing," he said.

"You look terrible. Are you feeling all right?"

Chuck nodded. He looked at me. He took my hand.

"Dawn," he started. Then I saw the *Variety* in his jacket pocket. My eye caught the headline on the first page which announced:

GARY LUCCHESI TO PARAMOUNT AS EXEC VEEP

The text of the article was stunning. It basically said Lucchesi would report directly to Tanen, which was a signal to the industry and to me that effectively I was no longer president of production.

I knew who Gary Lucchesi was. The day before I had left for my maternity leave, I had noticed his name on Ned's appointment book.

But even before then, his name had been mentioned around Paramount a number of times. Not only that, but Chuck had recommended Lucchesi to me for a job. I was looking for a new senior executive. Kirkpatrick had left when it became clear he was never going to unseat me to become head of production. So his job was open. Lucchesi called Chuck about the Paramount job, and at the same time had also asked if Chuck would introduce him to Tom Pollock, who was chairman of Universal.

Chuck, being Chuck, said, "Sure," and then suggested to me that I meet him.

I said: "I don't think he's really that great, Chuck." This was another instance, in my view, of a pig who would have to be taught to sing. Lucchesi had been an undistinguished junior studio executive at Tri-Star, a man with a ready smile for his superiors, sort of reminiscent of those little dolls in the backs of cars whose heads turn from left to right with static grins on their faces. Prior to that, he had been an agent.

But Chuck said, "You should really meet him. I think he might make a good executive."

I agreed, but somehow we just couldn't pin down a date to meet. It seemed Lucchesi had just used Chuck to cover his bases by requesting the meeting.

I confronted Ned. And Ned denied it.

At one point, Chuck called Lucchesi and asked him straight out, "What's going on?" But he denied that he was involved with Tanen and Mancuso behind my back. He denied it until the very end.

My hospital room was wall-to-wall flowers. The ceiling was covered with bright helium balloons. Nurses and aides kept coming in with more and more gifts from friends and relatives and business associates.

Chuck sat at the edge of my hospital bed, holding my hand. Rebecca slept soundly in my arms. I suddenly remembered that day, in the second-floor ladies room at Paramount, when I heard the two secretaries saying I was finished.

Six months had passed. And they had killed me.

My eyes filled with tears. I looked at my family, the family I had waited for all my life. Nothing and no one was going to take one minute of joy away from me. Away from us. I didn't cry. And I never cried about it after that.

Besides, at that moment Dean Paul Martin, Jr., walked in. He was our first visitor. He gazed at Rebecca. "You know," said Dino, "she looks exactly like me."

He stayed with us long past visiting hours. Finally, he got up to leave; he had to get up early the following morning. Dean was a jet pilot in the Air National Guard and he had to get up for practice maneuvers. More than anything, he loved to fly. He was the real Top Gun.

Rebecca, at three days old, already hated the phone.

There were calls of congratulations about Rebecca and calls of condolence about my job. But every time I picked up the phone, Rebecca started to wail. So I stopped answering the phone.

Chuck stayed in the hospital, taking care of me, the baby and all of our visitors. But he was indignant. He finally called Lucchesi.

"How could you do this? I want to understand. I understand why you went after the position, but why would you use me as a beard with my wife?"

Lucchesi said, "It's only business, Chuck. It's only business."

Some of this is just Hollywood style. After all, this is the town where executives used to find out that they were fired when they'd pull into the lot in the morning and their name was painted over in their parking spot. "It's only business."

Chuck went to work on Friday for half a day. I was ready to take my baby home, but they wanted to keep us a day or two more.

That evening, when Chuck came from the office to see us, the color had drained from his face. He told me that Dean was missing.

Early that morning, Dean, their friend Scott Sandler, and Dean's eleven-year-old son Alex had gone out to the National Guard airfield for Dean's practice maneuvers. Alex and Scott had brought a video camera and taped Dean's takeoff. It was magnificent, even though there was a low ceiling and it was overcast.

Three jets took off. Dean was in the middle. Because of the low ceiling, the pilot of the first jet asked permission to fly into commercial air space. His request was denied. He did a power turn and went back to the base.

Dean requested to fly into commercial air space. He, too, was denied permission, and made a power turn back to the base.

The pilot of the third jet was also denied permission, but ignored the air controller and went into commercial space anyway.

The pilots of the first and third jets returned to the base. Dean didn't.

Scott and Alex waited till dark for Dean to return to the base. Then they called Dean's family and Chuck.

There was nothing we could do but wait.

I had been home from the hospital a few days when Frank Mancuso came to visit.

I was still smarting from the betrayal and from my surgery. It was the first time I had walked downstairs.

Frank was waiting for me in my living room. He congratulated me, kissed me on both cheeks, and after a little small talk said, "I want you to come back as head of production after your maternity leave."

I said: "You must be kidding. How could you want me to come back? You let Ned torture me. You let him humiliate me."

And he said, "I can make this work. Let me talk to Ned."

And I said, "No, Frank. I'm not coming back."

He said, "Please. Let me just talk to Ned about it. When he gets crazy like this, I don't know how to handle him."

But I wasn't really listening. My mind had wandered. I was thinking about Dean, who was still missing. Chuck had been on the phone constantly for days while the search went on. He couldn't sleep. He was devastated. Neither of us was willing to give up hope of finding him.

I heard Frank say that he didn't know how to handle Ned. But I didn't care. Finally Frank left. He never called me again.

To this day, I don't really know what happened, for

sure. What I've been told is that Ned was telling Frank that he needed an executive he could talk to, and he couldn't talk to me. I'm also told he kept telling Frank that nobody knew whether I'd really come back after I had the baby.

And, of course, many people would have kept the title—and the money—and swallowed their pride. It's a time-honored way of surviving near the center of power in corporate America, and in Hollywood.

I still blame Frank Mancuso much more than I blame Ned. I trusted him. He pretended to be something to me that he wasn't.

Of course, I know that some would say that's bullshit, that Ned Tanen is the one who really did the dirty work. But Frank's betrayal was more personal.

I had worked with him for almost ten years. I had been to his house for Christmas dinner. His wife, daughter and daughter-in-law had given me my baby shower. Why didn't he tell me if he was unhappy with me?

There is a management style that basically leaves the system to run itself. That was Frank Mancuso's approach and it was a mistake. Frank was a non-confrontational guy. He found it impossible to give people bad news, or to enforce unpopular decisions. His management style paralyzed Paramount.

What had been my responsibility in all this? What had been my role in this drama? It would take me a while to figure it out.

* * *

They found remnants of Dean's plane a week later. He had hit a mountain at full throttle and most of the plane had disintegrated on impact. There was no body.

Within one week, my husband saw the birth of his child and the death of his oldest and closest friend.

When I first met Bruce Rubin, who wrote *Ghost,* he talked about the Hindu notion of growth, which is that the only way gods could grow is to come to earth as humans and experience love and pain. That there is no growth without love or pain.

I was no god. But I was learning that lesson.

BOOK
THREE

TEMPERED
STEEL

16

HIGH
ANXIETY

1987. BILLY JOEL IS BACK IN THE U.S.S.R. THE TOP SONGS are George Michael's "Faith," Heart's "Alone" and Whitney Houston's "I Wanna Dance with Somebody (Who Loves Me)." Paramount ranked No. 1 at the box office, and set a new high for profits—over $600 million. Even better than Diller–Eisner's best year, 1984. The profits reflected many of the movies I had helped put into play, including *Top Gun, Star Trek IV, The Golden Child* and *Pretty in Pink*. When I left on maternity leave, *The Accused, The Untouchables, Beverly Hills Cop II, Fatal Attraction* and *Ghost* were all in the pipeline.

Rebecca was three months old, and she was still breast-feeding, something I'd now grown quite accustomed to. So while she was napping, I decided to go shopping at Neiman Marcus. I had lost some weight, not enough to buy clothes, but enough to buy a pair of shoes. My feet were back to normal.

My mother and father had come to stay with us for a while, to get to know their granddaughter. I had never seen them so happy. As a family, we had never been so happy together.

I was having a ball. Lucy's baby, Sarah, had been born about three weeks before Rebecca, so we were new mothers together. What surprised me was how good I was at being a mother, how easy it was to segue into a whole other life, how much I loved that new life. Rebecca was the happiest baby in the world. And I had no anxiety. This was the first time since before my Pappagallo job that I hadn't worked, and for the first time in my life, I loved Sunday nights.

Lucy and I were amazed at how full our days were. We went to the park and climbed barefoot into the sand box with Rebecca and Sarah. We spent hours pushing them in infant swings and in strollers down suburban streets. I began to notice how many strollers there actually were. How many babies. How many women were on the streets, during the day, during the week, with their children. I was one of them. And I was happy about it.

I was so attached to Rebecca that until that moment I hadn't been able to leave her for an hour. As I got off the Neiman's escalator on the second floor, I stopped in the lingerie department, gazing longingly at a sexy teddy, wondering when and if I would ever be able to fit this body into that teddy. I moved quickly on to shoes.

The salesman was just slipping my foot into a suede loafer when suddenly I heard, from the other side of the floor, a baby's cry. I knew it wasn't my baby, she was safely at home.

But my breasts didn't know that. Without warning, they filled with milk, leaked through my nursing bra and milk spurted out of my shirt.

The salesman was mortified. He was sitting with my foot in his hand, but he couldn't take his stunned eyes off my chest. He stuttered, "H-Ho-How do they feel?" meaning the shoes. But I'd lost interest in shoes. I knew I had to get home. I knew Rebecca was awake. Clearly, it was not time for me to separate from her.

There was an expression going around Hollywood at the time: They can kill you but they can't eat you. Paramount had killed me. They had taken away my authority, that was clear. But they couldn't take away my drive. And I was starting to feel that I wanted to go back to work. I just didn't know what I wanted to do next.

Typically, when an executive at a studio steps down or is pushed out, the studio gives said executive a consolation prize. This prize takes the form of an "overall production deal." And in the trade papers, the same announcement always seems to appear:

SO AND SO, FORMER HEAD OF PRODUCTION (SENIOR EXECUTIVE, HEAD OF STUDIO), HAS STEPPED DOWN (RESIGNED, BEEN REPLACED, BEEN THROWN OUT), TO

PURSUE (FULFILL) HIS (HER) LIFELONG DREAM OF BE-
COMING AN INDEPENDENT PRODUCER (GOING INDIE
PROD).

So I was going to pursue (fulfill) my lifelong dream
of going indie prod. My consolation prize was a great
production deal at Paramount.

I had to choose office space. I drove onto the
Paramount lot for the first time in six months. The
guard handed me a guest pass, and insisted I put it in
the front window where it could be seen. Of course, I
no longer had my own parking space.

In fact, I no longer belonged there at all. Walking
across the lot, I felt vulnerable. And embarrassed.
Here was the lot I had grown up on, the lot on which I
had worked for almost ten years. I felt like an outsider.
I knew this was no longer home for me.

Ray Stark was a people collector. Like David
Geffen, he kept track of people who impressed him.
He had called me the day after the publication of the
"Flashfight" article in the *Los Angeles Times,* the
piece about who should get the credit for *Flashdance.*

"You sound interesting," he had said. "I want to
know you."

"Okay, Mr. Stark," I said.

"Ray," he said.

What I got was an ally who gave me support for
years. What he got was someone who wanted to be
good to him. We became friends. And we stayed
friends, through my tenure at Columbia. Ray had

been collecting people for forty years, and that collection was as impressive as his art collection, which was extraordinary. In the garden at his home were Henry Moores, Alexander Calders, and a Giacometti, among others.

Ray started out as an agent and became one of Hollywood's most successful and colorful producers. He willed many films into existence, not the least of which was *Funny Girl*. At the age of seventy-something, Ray Stark was still wielding more power than most men half his age. He had also been a lifelong friend of the investment banker Herbert Allen, who had a substantial financial interest in Columbia.

Ray called me when I was on maternity leave, once it had become publicly clear what had happened to me at Paramount. He said, "I've been discussing you for the Columbia job with Victor Kaufman [chairman of Columbia], Mike Ovitz and Herbert." I also knew that Melnick had been talking me up to Ray (whether I liked it or not).

Apparently, this had started when Chuck and his friend, C.A.A. agent Todd Smith, were having lunch. David Puttnam had just resigned or had been pushed out of Columbia (see "consolation prize" on page 243), and they were discussing who was going to fill the Columbia presidency. At the top of the list would be the people who had already had the job of running a studio and succeeded (there was no one available). Then there would be people who had run a studio and failed (a couple of those people were available). Then there would be people who hadn't yet done the job, but who had had success as heads of production.

Todd said, "What about Dawn?"

Chuck answered, "Maybe. But she's gun-shy." Better than anyone, Chuck knew that I would not and could not campaign for the job because of what I had just been through. That if I was ever going to take a job like that, they were going to have to really want me. Otherwise, I couldn't possibly stomach going back into corporate politics. Chuck thought about it and said to Todd, "I'll talk to Dawn. You talk to Ronnie."

Ronnie, of course, was C.A.A. agent (new president) Ron Meyer. Todd did talk to Ronnie, Ronnie spoke to Ray, and Ray called me.

Ray said that he and Mike and Herbert had been talking and would I be interested in meeting Victor Kaufman?

I didn't know Victor Kaufman. But I had heard of him. He had been very successful in starting Tri-Star, the only new movie studio other than Orion to be classified as a "major" since the major studios were originally founded.

Herbert Allen, whom everyone called just "Herbert," is an investment banker quietly worth an enormous amount of money, a man with great taste in everything from art and houses to literature. (By the way, he's single, too.) He lives his life better than anyone I've ever met, his way. Herbert was at work hours before anyone else; he was also asleep hours before anyone else so if you wanted to have dinner with him, you had to be prepared to eat at six o'clock. His hobbies are as important to him as his work; travel, fly fishing in Alaska, and the baseball team he plays on with his friend, a bartender from San Francisco. The team travels all over the world, representing middle-aged America. I aspired—and still do—to

246

live my life the way Herbert lives his, which is: He works to live. He does not live to work.

I met with Victor, and then with Herbert, and then with Don Keough, president of Coca-Cola and the very first industrial giant I had ever met. Don is larger than life—a big bear of a guy with silver hair and wonderful warmth. He has that rare gift of walking into a room and making everyone feel comfortable. He sees it as his job. I felt an immediate connection with these people.

Yet, after all of my meetings, when Victor called and asked, "How would you like to run Columbia?" I was still very ambivalent. In the first place, I knew that this would be a tough job. Maybe an impossible job. Second, I was in paradise with my daughter and Chuck, and I knew if I took on this more-than-full-time job, it would affect my family. Finally, I was still licking my wounds from the Paramount debacle.

On the other hand, I did know it was the call of my life. To be offered the whole enchilada, if I wanted it, was an affirmation of everything I had done until then. It was proof to me that even if the Paramount people didn't value me, there were others who did.

Victor Kaufman was definitely a factor in my taking the job. He is a thoroughly original businessman. He's tall and handsome and dresses conservatively in proper, dark pin-striped suits by day. But in his spare time, he and his (equally smart, highly educated) wife, Loretta, love to dress up in sixties outfits and go to sock hops and dance the lindy. And they're great at it.

So Victor's attributes include an unusual and appealing mixture of wicked business acumen and full-blown whimsy.

He was the perfect liaison to the Coca-Cola people,

who owned Columbia at the time. Victor understood how important the idea of family was to them, and fiscal responsibility, but above all, he understood he was in charge of a floundering business that had to be quickly turned around.

Just to give you an idea of the way he operates, when I was offered the job, Victor and the Coca-Cola people insisted on a couple of things: one, that I have a nursery next to my office for Rebecca, and second, that I tell them what I needed in terms of personal help at home: they would do everything they could to find it and help me pay for it.

This was the proverbial offer I couldn't refuse. I had a feeling I could trust Victor. And it turned out I was right.

We met again at the Beverly Hills Hotel and the tone of our meetings made me lean in the direction of taking the job. But when he told me he was interviewing several people, I found myself half-wishing someone else would get it.

It was Chuck who finally convinced me to go ahead. Not for the money. Or the title. But because he understood that I needed to finish what I started, to prove to myself that I could run a studio. "You would be the first woman to head an entire motion picture corporation. How can you say no?" he asked me. He also felt that if I were able to do it, I would be operating with a level of confidence I'd never had before.

Ray called me. "Victor is very impressed with you," he said. "And I am now going to step aside and let Mike Ovitz take over, because you will need him to shape your deal. And then you will need him to help bring you projects when you run the studio."

I got to know Mike when he negotiated the deal for

me at Columbia with my lawyer Jake Bloom. Together, they negotiated me into a place of protection and security, a place I'd never been before; no one could be hired above me or below me without my approval . . . that is, unless the company was sold.

Later I would deal with Mike often. And I learned many important lessons from him. For example, if he didn't like the way a deal was being negotiated or if he didn't like the way a client was being handled, instead of saying, "How dare you treat my client this way?" or threatening or criticizing, he'd quietly say, "I'm confused." This invariably provoked the response—from me anyway—of wanting to help him. *It's a simple but very smart phrase: "I'm confused."*

I suspect Mike Ovitz, even at the beginning of his career, saw himself as one of the most powerful men in Hollywood. And he became that.

And he's cute. He runs C.A.A., one of Hollywood's most important talent agencies, like a commune: everyone is responsible for everyone else and everyone who works there respects him and loves him. Without exception. I called them Mike's Moonies.

We made the deal over a weekend. I still had misgivings, of course. I was now going to be a Youpeople big time. But as it turned out, Frank Mancuso had misgivings, too. Because I was still under contract to Paramount, Victor had to ask Frank for my release. Frank refused, unless Columbia agreed to pay Paramount hundreds of thousands of dollars in a reparation payment for me. I was baffled; Paramount didn't want me, but they wouldn't let me go. Victor paid.

* * *

I was so excited, I couldn't sleep the entire night before. I couldn't believe my good fortune. I was about to embark on the adventure of a lifetime.

My first day as president of Columbia Pictures, October 28, 1987, I got lost going to Burbank. And I ran out of gas. I probably should have seen this as symbolic, but I was too thrilled to be thinking about gasoline or about symbols.

I drove up to the guard gate on the Columbia lot and was about to identify myself when the guard interrupted me. "Welcome to Columbia, Ms. Steel," he said and escorted me to my new parking spot. I was so happy I hugged him.

Since my entire Hollywood tenure had been spent within the confines of Paramount, this was just like switching schools in the middle of the term. I walked into the building and introduced myself to another guard. This guard then escorted me upstairs to my office. As if on a receiving line, everyone stood in the doorway of their offices, waiting to get a look at their new boss. I literally met everyone right then and there in the hall. I'll never remember these names, I was telling myself. But I did.

Finally, I got to my own office, greeted my secretaries, closed the door, sat down, and twirled around in my chair. Is this great or what! I shrieked to myself. And then I started to laugh. "Oh my God, what do I do now?"

Gifts arrived, welcoming me to my new position. There was a crystal ball, to remind me of how scientific decision-making is in the movie business; a six-inch ceramic screw that Dan Melnick gave me to keep things in perspective; a four-foot-tall magic wand from my old friend Jim Wiatt, now president of

I.C.M.; a needlepoint pillow of the Columbia lady holding up a torch, courtesy of Ray Stark, to remind me that Columbia had the only female logo in the history of the movie business; and a bronze turkey that Ron Meyer sent which bore a plaque reading, "Please God, don't let me make any turkeys."

Columbia had had four or five administrations in the previous four or five years, and each administration had hired its own people without firing the previous administration's staff.

Steve Martin, who was voted best actor for *Roxanne* by the L.A. Film Critics that year, summed it up perfectly in his acceptance speech. To paraphrase:

Roxanne was green-lighted by studio head Guy McElwaine. While we were shooting the movie, Frank Price took over from Guy McElwaine. During the beginning of postproduction, Steve Sohmer took over from Frank Price. During the end of postproduction, David Puttnam took over from Steve Sohmer. And now, just in time for the video release, I'm happy to announce that Dawn Steel, who has taken over from David Puttnam, is the fifth studio head in charge of *Roxanne*.

Steve said it funnier than that, but the personnel problems resulting from all of these administrations was no joke. And one of my first jobs was the horrible task of downsizing Columbia. We had to cut overhead to make the company profitable. We also had to make hits.

One of my next jobs was to go over the slate of David Puttnam's projects and weed through what we wanted to make and what we didn't want to make. I knew that we had agreed we wouldn't cancel any of his movies already in production or anything that had been green-lighted; we would honor his commitments, whether we thought they'd make money for the studio or not. What I didn't know was that there were many movies in production that were esoteric, uncommercial and in languages other than English. In fact, one was in Serbo-Croatian, a language so obscure that it had to be subtitled in its native Yugoslavia!

I took David Puttnam to lunch to hear firsthand about the projects he had in the works and he was very gracious.

I respected him. He was a solid producer with an impressive résumé; his pictures included *The Mission, The Killing Fields* and one of my all-time favorites, *Chariots of Fire.* In Hollywood, he had a reputation for being both an outspoken outsider and someone who only worked on high-quality projects. He had generated big hopes when he first came to Columbia. The press had pegged him as someone who would fight the spiraling and inflated costs of making movies, a leader who would put egomaniacal stars in their place.

But Puttnam went too far too fast and he soon had a coup on his hands. Warren Beatty, Dustin Hoffman and Bill Murray were so incensed by Puttnam's high-handed attitude toward them that they refused to continue working at Columbia.

Reporters loved him for his "reverse snobbery," as *The Wall Street Journal* put it, because he wouldn't go to Hollywood power restaurants, rejected the

Mercedes that went along with his job, lived in a house that the press liked to describe as "modest," and had been married to the same woman for twenty-five years.

Of course, much of Puttnam's trouble in the movie business was just the usual Hollywood backbiting and -stabbing. But he had also come in swinging at Ovitz and the power of the agencies. He made it clear, from the get-go, that he was waging an artistic and moral crusade against Hollywood. He announced that he would not make big deals with movie stars or big directors. And though this was irresistible to the Hollywood press, it was highly antagonistic to the Hollywood establishment.

Puttnam also had very real problems running Columbia. He had never headed a large U.S. company before, let alone a huge studio with a release schedule of at least fifteen movies a year and an annual combined production and marketing budget of more than $400 million.

Neither had I. Puttnam knew exactly what I would be facing, and at that lunch he was extremely sympathetic to me.

I recruited a terrific staff. There were some talented people already there: Michael Nathanson, now head of production at Columbia; Gareth Wigan, the most diplomatic of executives, now an executive vice-president at Columbia; Barry Sabbath, a funny, outspoken, former creative executive whom I promoted; the very gifted Amy Pascal, whom I brought over from Fox and who is now an executive vice-president at Columbia; Rob Fried, an executive who knew a great idea when he heard one, came from Orion; Stephanie Allain, a woman with a great nose for material, who rose rapidly from reader to creative executive, and who is now a senior vice-president at Columbia; and Gary Martin, the very great head of physical production, who watched my back like a hawk.

We had our work cut out for us. When I arrived, Columbia was second to last in box office share among the studios, number 8 out of 9. The good news was I had nowhere to go but up. The bad news was I had nowhere to go but up.

The first thing we had to do was to put *Ghostbusters II* back together. (The first *Ghostbusters* had made over $200 million.) I say back together because both Bill Murray and C.A.A., who represented him; the writers Lowell Ganz and Babaloo Mandel; the producer-director Ivan Reitman; and the actors Dan Aykroyd and Harold Ramis, had been offended and alienated by Puttnam.

I was in a position to clean up these relationships. Quickly. I wish I could say that it was more difficult than it was, but all of our goals were the same: we all wanted to make this movie. And with a minimum of effort and a lot of good will, *Ghostbusters II* went back on track.

One down. *Karate Kid III* was next. This one was not difficult either. David Puttnam thought these sequels were just crass and commercial movies. To us, they were unmined gems.

Two down. And then the phone rang.

It was Marty Scorsese, asking me to unlock the legal logjam blocking the restoration of one of the greatest movies ever made. "What's the problem on *Lawrence of Arabia*? Why are you holding it up, Dawn?"

"What are you talking about?" I said.

"You're in the middle of a lawsuit," he told me.

"Wait a minute," I said. "Are we suing someone or is someone suing us?"

He laughed. "You better get into this," he said. "The original negative from 1962 is corroding."

It turned out there was some arcane, ridiculous legal problem buried deep inside the company. Once I found it, I was able to jump-start the process of restoring *Lawrence of Arabia*.

Victor and I agreed that the restoration of *Lawrence of Arabia* would bring prestige to the studio. I wanted to send a signal to the community that we were committed to making commercial and quality movies; I did not believe those two concepts were mutually exclusive.

The most exciting part of it for me was that David Lean came with the package and he supervised the work. I got to watch him, ask him questions and spend time with a master.

One of the most amazing moments came the day Peter O'Toole re-recorded some of his dialogue on a looping stage in England, putting his voice over a face thirty years younger. He was heartrending in front of the microphone, looking up at himself on screen as the spectacularly beautiful Lawrence. We got it all on film, and the juxtaposition of the younger and older O'Tooles was one of the most poignant things I'd ever seen.

I shut down the studio on a Friday afternoon and bussed everyone to the Academy of Motion Picture Arts and Sciences, so that our employees could see the restored *Lawrence of Arabia*. It was a great and moving day.

On opening night, there was a star-studded Hollywood premiere. Klieg lights, cameras, movie stars.

This was no rubber-chicken event. Everyone else had been seated. I walked David Lean to the stage, our arms linked together.

On stage was the original cast, Peter O'Toole, Omar Sharif, and Anthony Quinn, along with Marty Scorsese; Steven Spielberg; the editor, Annie Coates; the director of photography, Freddy Young; and the two restorers of the film, Robert Harris and Jim Painten. David Lean talked about how he had worked with the great gamblers of the entertainment industry, men who were not afraid to take big risks: Louis B. Mayer, Jack Warner, Sam Spiegel, Harry Cohn. And then he said that he was thrilled to have had the pleasure of working with another mogul, another gambler, a real risk-taker, and that *her* name was Dawn Steel.

Lawrence of Arabia, a twenty-seven-year-old epic, was a big hit. Again.

17

MUTINY AT MOMMY AND ME

1988. THE DEMOCRATS CHOOSE MICHAEL DUKAKIS AND Lloyd Bentsen as their presidential candidates. The Republicans choose Vice-President Bush and Dan Quayle. Cher wins an Oscar the day before Sonny is elected mayor of Palm Springs. The Beatles are inducted into the Rock 'n' Roll Hall of Fame. The top songs are INXS's "Need You Tonight," Chicago's "Look Away" and Steve Winwood's "Roll with It." *Driving Miss Daisy* wins the Pulitzer Prize for drama. The big movies are *Rain Man, Who Framed Roger Rabbit?, Coming to America, Crocodile Dundee II* and *Twins.*

Chuck went into production on two movies that were being made out of town, way out of town. Australia, for one. And New Orleans.

This was no coincidence. He had been wonderfully steadfast through all my troubles and had been involved with every single aspect of my getting the Columbia job. But now he started feeling that he was in danger of losing himself.

So he went away to make his own movies. He had to go. (But did it have to be Australia?!)

It was an incredibly stressful time for us. Intimacy is the easiest and quickest thing to lose in a marriage and we were losing ours.

I do remember this as a period in which I was so in tune with our child that the world seemed to revolve around that connection. When I took Rebecca to get a shot and she cried, I cried too. My attachment to her was so powerful that I felt connected not only to my own, but to every child I saw.

For the two and a half years that I was at Columbia, I insisted on having "Rebecca time" in the morning, from six to eight. I didn't take calls. I never "did" breakfast anymore because I had breakfast with her. So from six to eight we were together, and as we got older we would dress together, put on our makeup together, and take a shower together.

Coming home from the office for dinner with Rebecca was the hard part. I stopped at the house to spend an hour with her, have dinner with her, and then I would go back out again to a business dinner or a sneak preview of one of our movies. I never missed a night with her unless I was out of town, and I was never out of town for more than two days without her. Part of Columbia's gift to me was that I could travel with Rebecca and our nanny, Marilyn Mordecai. Marilyn made my life possible.

As did Victor and his friend and second-in-command, Lou Korman, whom I would eventually report to. Lou was the corporate COO, and a feminist, although I don't know that this is the word he would use. What a great combination, a feminist corporate executive who's a man. It's interesting that both Lou and Victor had great wives. These are two men with a very progressive point of view. I was really lucky.

Rebecca became a fixture at Columbia. She learned to walk on the two flights of stairs up to my office. Her nursery, attached to my office, was not only a playground for her, but also a haven for me.

When we started toilet training Rebecca, she developed an interesting habit: she insisted on taking off every stitch of clothing she had on. Everything. When this happened during the day I would usually assist in the undressing and stay in the nursery bathroom to coach and cheer and help her get her clothes back on.

She must have had some telepathy with Don Keough, because he would inevitably call during one of our efforts. I would ask my assistant to tell his office to please hold on while Rebecca went through her potty process. How long could it take?!

When it seemed appropriate, I'd ask:

"Rebecca, are you finished yet?"

"No, Mommy."

"Rebecca, how about putting your shirt back on?"

"I'm not ready Mommy."

"Rebecca, is it time yet?"

"No, Mommy, I'm not finished."

"Okay, honey, I'll come back."

Leaving the door open, I'd start walking back toward my office when I'd hear:

"Mommy? I'm ready!"

First things first. Don Keough had to wait. And I knew *he* would understand.

When Rebecca was almost two and ready to socialize, I found a Mommy and Me class that took place on Saturdays. It was the only one in all of L.A., which baffled me about what the other women with jobs did if they wanted to participate in their children's first group encounters.

This class was at the Stephen S. Wise Temple and it was part of something called The Parenting Center because it was for both parents—it wasn't just for Mommy and Me. Because the class was on Saturday, it was possible for both parents to show up. What a wonderfully enlightened place this is, I thought.

One day the headmistress walked in to announce that they had created a music and dance class for the children and that it would be held on Wednesdays at three o'clock. She paused and she said, "Remember, ladies, no caregivers."

My hand shot up. "What do you mean, no caregivers? You know we're all working parents here."

She looked at me with disdain and said, "Take the day off, Miss Steel."

That began the mutiny at Mommy and Me. We elected one of our more articulate and calm parents to speak to one of the rabbis. She told him our story. Without missing a beat he said, "This is not a problem for us at Stephen S. Wise Temple. This is the most affluent congregation in the United States and our women don't have to work."

Huh?

That day, many of the mommies of Mommy and Me left. We made other arrangements.

Often, I made bimonthly flights to New York, and I would usually take Rebecca.

One day, when our flight was delayed, I went into the lounge to wait. Rebecca, who was a year old, was riding on my hip.

And there, in the lounge, was Ned Tanen, watching a *Jeopardy* rerun. It was the first time I had seen Ned since leaving Paramount to go on maternity leave, the first I had spoken to him since he called on the morning of Rebecca's birth to congratulate me.

I walked over to him. "You never met Rebecca," I said.

He looked at Rebecca for a long time, then back up at me. A big tear rolled out of his left eye, and he said: "It was Frank."

My typical day began at five o'clock in the morning when I would finish reading scripts by the side of Rebecca's bed until she woke up at seven. It was thrilling to find a script that I loved, something I desperately wanted to make. And when I found one, my day was made by seven A.M.

If I didn't have a script to finish, I had notes to make on those I had read. And if I'd finished my notes, I went downstairs to exercise.

After mornings with Rebecca, I'd arrive at the office at nine-thirty. The phone calls had started long before

I got there. By ten o'clock I was in a staff meeting, and depending on the day of the week, it was either a production, marketing/distribution or business-affairs meeting.

By eleven-thirty, I might be in a meeting with an executive about a particular movie or problem. By twelve, I was meeting with a director I was trying to seduce back to the studio.

By twelve forty-five, I'd get in my car and drive across town to a lunch meeting with an agent, a producer, a writer or a movie star. While driving, I'd start to return the phone calls that had started before I ever arrived at my office.

At two-thirty, I was back in the car, returning more phone calls, the calls from early morning, from mid-morning, plus East Coast and Europe calls that came in during lunch.

At two forty-five, I was back in the office. Inevitably, there were people waiting to see me, executives with personal problems, political problems and/or production problems. In between, I returned and made more phone calls.

At three-thirty, there could be a meeting with someone I was trying to bring to the studio. At four-thirty, there was a script meeting with an executive, writer, producer and/ or director. At five o'clock, there were selected dailies of the movies we were shooting. And if I hadn't finished watching them by six-thirty, the rest were put on tape for me to watch later at home.

At six-thirty, I'd jump into my car and return more phone calls on my drive home. The call sheet numbered one hundred to one hundred and fifty calls a day. And I always felt it was very important to return every call. *The lesson here is people remember when you don't call them back.*

I'd go home to be with Rebecca. If I didn't have a business dinner or a sneak preview of one of our movies, I had to go to a black-tie event. There was at least one of them a week, honoring someone from our industry. I went out of respect for the talent involved and my counterparts at the other studios. So Rebecca would keep me company while I washed off my makeup, put on new makeup, dressed in black tie, kissed her good-bye and shot out the door.

That's where men really have it good: they just put on a tux and go.

After I got home at ten-thirty, I would sit on the chair next to Rebecca's bed. Watching her sleep dissolved all the stress in my body.

Then I would get up, either finish watching the dailies, or read a script, wash my face and fall into bed at eleven-thirty.

But the part of my workday that made me the happiest was when I was closest to the actual making of a movie.

I spent a lot of my time packing and unpacking. If I couldn't take Rebecca with me, I tried to keep my trips down to three days.

Which was impossible when I flew to Thailand to show De Palma and his crew my support for *Casualties of War*. When I got there Michael Fox and Sean Penn—who had been going stir crazy, stuck in this little town—insisted on taking me to a snake-blood drinking place. You would have thought it would have been Sean who jumped into that pit with the snake. It wasn't. It was Michael. I went home. Quickly.

Then there was the time I went to Dallas to have dinner with a superstar who was shooting a movie there, someone I wanted to do one of our movies, a man I found to be unbearably handsome. But because I was happily married, I just wanted to make a movie with him. I didn't want to make love with him.

We had finished dinner and he was walking me to my car as we discussed movies of his that I loved. Suddenly, he pushed me against a wall of a darkened corner of the building. He unzipped his pants and took out his penis. I was so taken off guard that I started to laugh. "What are you doing?" I yelled. "Put that back. *Right* now!" He was so surprised that he laughed. He zipped up his pants and finished walking me to my car. We never made a movie together. But we did stay friends.

Some of business was fun. One night, for example, Sean Penn and Madonna came to my house for dinner. This was an evening I was looking forward to. I had been working on developing some properties with Madonna and I had met Sean right after he did *Taps*. I was very fond of them both.

We were still living in the Cecil Beaton pool house. There was a gate and there wasn't a long walk between the gate and the main house. Madonna and Sean arrived and rang the bell at the gate. I opened the gate electronically from the house and then waited for them to come up the walk. Minutes went by and they didn't arrive. I decided there must be something wrong.

I walked out of the house, down the front path, through the gate. It was like the attack of the killer bees. Paparazzi swarmed around Sean and Madonna, who were incarcerated in their car.

I was so incensed that the press had violated my privacy and the privacy of my guests that I actually grabbed one of the photographers by the scruff of his neck and pulled him off the car. "Get out of here!" I yelled. He slugged me and I hit the ground by the side of Sean's car. I was in a brawl in my own driveway.

Sean saw me go down. He barreled out of the car to make sure I was okay. Then he took off after the photographers as they ran down the road, their cameras flapping in the wind. I was forever grateful to Sean.

We finally went inside and sat down; I was shaken. Over dinner, I said to Madonna, "How do you live like this?" She said that it normally didn't bother her except for the day they followed her to the shrink. They got out of their car when she got out of her car. They followed her into the elevator and they followed her down the hallway to her shrink's office. I told Madonna she should have made *them* pay for the session.

I was having my own problems with the press. They blamed me for David Puttnam's demise. They blamed me for the fact that his movies didn't open, accusing me of purposely tanking them.

And then the Sony rumors began.

Suddenly, there was talk that the Sony Corporation was interested in buying Columbia. This was the first time anyone had heard of a Japanese company wanting to buy an American movie studio. There was a lot of discomfort about this: the Japanese referred to the movie studios as suppliers of "software." We thought of ourselves quite differently; we were "creators of culture." Not just software.

The entertainment press was fascinated with this culture clash. And because they were already down on me for "killing David Puttnam's children," they loved fanning the flames of any rumor that surfaced about me. One of which was that when Sony bought Columbia, I was dead.

From that moment on, every time I replaced an assistant, it was news. Bad news. Every time I burped it made headlines. Every time I lost my temper, it was man bites dog. Or in my case, woman bites man. The press was on me like white on rice.

18

HAVING
IT ALL

1989. THE EIGHTIES ARE ALMOST OVER.

By now, there was absolutely no difference between my work life and my personal life.

Chuck and I wanted to buy a house. The Cecil Beaton pool house had become too small for all of us.

On weekends when he would come home from Australia and New Orleans—I don't know how he did it—we went house-hunting. One day we found an old house built in the 1930s. The property was not in good shape. There was no grass, only weeds, but the house was exquisite and the view looked like a movie shot of a Los Angeles panorama.

We met John Calley, who was the owner of the house and former vice chairman of Warner Brothers. He had retired a couple of years before.

"What are you working on?" he asked. I described our current projects and asked, "What about you? What are you working on?"

He said he had come out of retirement to produce a movie that Mike Nichols was going to direct based on Carrie Fisher's book *Postcards from the Edge,* and that Meryl Streep was going to play the lead. He said the movie was just falling out at MGM, where it had been developed.

I looked at Chuck and said, "Do you want to buy this house?"

And he said, "Yes, do you?"

And I said, "Yes, but I also want to buy this movie."

We got our house with its beautiful view, and Columbia got *Postcards from the Edge.*

The screenwriters went on strike on March 7, 1988. This was a devastating occurrence for everyone, especially for a new studio head who had no inventory. This stopped me dead. I couldn't get anything written. I couldn't get anything rewritten.

I focused on releasing Puttnam's thirty-three movies, a few of which I liked. Some of the people who had made their movies at Columbia were old friends, and I had relationships with some that were important to me, so I didn't want to leave them hanging out to dry. Dan Melnick had produced *Punchline;* David Mamet had written and directed *Things Change;* Ron Howard had produced *Vibes* with Cyndi Lauper; Jimmy Woods was the star of *True Believer.* And there were others.

We worked hard and spent a lot of money, but no matter what we did, these movies "did not open"— Hollywood parlance for bad initial box office. They did not make money.

I had a lot to learn about marketing and distribution. I made mistakes. I hired some wrong people, and then I hired some right people: Buffy Shutt and Kathy Jones moved three thousand miles to take over marketing for Columbia Pictures. Once they got there, it wasn't long before I began to feel cautiously optimistic about our marketing. And our future.

Many of the filmmakers who had worked with Puttnam were hostile and angry toward me. And I didn't blame them. You couldn't have dreamed up two more disparate executives than David Puttnam and me.

Among them was Spike Lee. He did not like me. No way. No how. After I saw the rough cut of his movie *School Daze,* I was excited about the movie that I saw inside the movie he had made. It was a great idea about discrimination within the black community, about the conflict between light-skinned people of color and dark-skinned people of color. It was a tremendously original and audacious concept for a musical. So when I met Spike for the first time (he had only made one movie prior to this), I said that I thought this movie was completely wonderful and I suggested some changes I thought would make the movie better. He didn't like any of them. His reaction, or nonreaction, made me uncomfortable. So, by way of making friendly small talk, I asked him what was the significance of the credits on his film.

The credits for *School Daze* read:

COLUMBIA PICTURES PRESENTS
FORTY ACRES AND A MULE
FILM WORKS
PRODUCTION
A SPIKE LEE JOINT
SCHOOL DAZE

A conventional director might have used the credit "A Spike Lee Film." But not Spike. So I asked him what it all meant—Forty Acres and A Mule and A Spike Lee Joint.

This was apparently a mistake. Spike was angry. He didn't answer me but I could've sworn that I heard him mutter under his breath, "White, bitch, ho."

I thought—No, he didn't say that! But just in case he did, I said, under my breath: "Uh unh. White, bitch, *Jew* ho."

Sometime later, I learned that the name of Spike's production company, FORTY ACRES AND A MULE, was a reference to what was given each slave when he was freed from bondage. I never did learn what SPIKE LEE JOINT meant.

Spike didn't like the way we marketed *School Daze*. Even though the movie was profitable and was one of the few movies that made money for the studio, he never came around.

Which was disappointing because one of my big jobs was to win talent back to Columbia—good directors, producers, writers and actors.

I went right to the top. I signed Madonna to an overall deal. I signed Spielberg to a development deal. And I wanted Michael Douglas.

Michael was the most successful actor-producer in town. He had been the producer of *Romancing the Stone, Jewel of the Nile, The China Syndrome* and *One Flew Over the Cuckoo's Nest,* among others. And, of course, with *Fatal Attraction,* he had become an even more successful leading man. If I could get Michael to bring his production company over to work with us, it would show that Columbia was back in business, big time, with mainstream Hollywood. And that deal would attract others like it.

I set out to seduce Michael Douglas. I would call him every day or every other day. I sent flowers. I took him out for drinks. I took him out to dinner. I introduced him to David Lean. In the Jeffrey Katzenberg scheme of things, when I couldn't get in the front door, I tried the back.

Not that this was a great hardship for me. Michael is funny and smart and endearing. And spending time with him was a lot more fun than having business affairs meetings in my office.

Romancing the Michael, I used to call it. Michael, who, like all of us, had been burnt by people in our business and, like all of us, had been rejected, responded to the friendship and admiration I offered him.

What I also had to offer Michael was a home, a place where his talent would be nurtured.

Several months after I began this campaign, to get talent back to Columbia, a golden opportunity fell into my lap. *The Last Emperor,* released by Columbia, directed by Bernardo Bertolucci, was up for nine Academy Awards. It looked to me like a good bet for a clean sweep of the Oscars.

Before I tell you about the night I threw the party for Bernardo Bertolucci and *The Last Emperor,* let me tell you what was at stake:

Columbia was still number eight out of the nine studios listed in *Variety's* box office share. The press was waiting for me to fail, as were a lot of Hollywood nay-sayers and detractors. The aforementioned writers' strike had shut me down. My bosses had put enormous faith in me to relight the Columbia torch, and I wasn't going to disappoint them. And as a woman in this job, I had a lot to prove.

Here's the scene: It was the night before the 1988 Academy Awards. It was a Sunday evening. The party was at my home. I was determined to make every single guest feel at home. And as Barry Diller had done to me years before, I stood at the front door and greeted every one of them personally, all two hundred of them.

This party was so important to Coca-Cola, that Don Keough and his *boss,* Roberto Goizueta, and their wives, Mickey and Olga, had flown all the way from Atlanta for the evening.

And the same was true for Columbia. Victor and Lou and Loretta and Sharon had flown in from New York earlier that day.

The food was fantastic, the setting was magazine-perfect, the lighting was done by a master, *The Last Emperor*'s Academy Award–winning cinematographer Vittorio Storaro, and I was a complete wreck.

The guests started to arrive. Arnold Schwarzenegger was first. Then Sean Connery. Jane Fonda. Bette Midler. Penny Marshall. Carrie Fisher. Glenn

Close. Kevin Costner. Michael Douglas. Madonna. Patrick Swayze. Mike Nichols. Rob Reiner and his soon-to-be wife, Michelle, came with Billy Crystal and his wife, Janis. We had just begun working on the release of Rob's movie *When Harry Met Sally,* which had been written by my friend Nora Ephron.

Word was radioed up that Al Pacino had arrived. I went to greet him. "Al!" I yelled warmly. Only the man walking toward me was not Al Pacino. It was Dustin Hoffman with his wife Lisa! Al and Dustin don't even look alike. I tried to cover quickly. "Allllisa!" I yelled, and hugged them both.

On the long steps leading from the living room to the pool were the funniest people in our business. It was the comedy stairs: Robin Williams, Billy Crystal, Richard Dreyfuss, Penny Marshall, Carrie Fisher, Steve Martin, Rob Reiner, Richard Pryor and Tom Hanks all riffing and making each other laugh. And that is some tough audience.

There was Sean Connery, flirting with my friend Katherine Reback.

There was Shirley MacLaine reading Patrick Swayze's palm while a small crowd looked on. They all wanted their palms to be read next.

Dustin was ferreting out the chef to find out who did the food. Steve Martin gave me a hug and said he was never going to leave.

This certainly beat selling toilet paper. Even in my high-anxiety state, this night was magic. My husband Chuck was at my side. Our beautiful Rebecca was asleep upstairs. Standing in my own living room, for one brief moment, I thought, "I have it all."

The following night, *The Last Emperor* became the

first movie since *Gigi* to win an Oscar for every category in which it was nominated.

Columbia was getting back on track.

And now, a couple of years after I had arrogantly declared to Lynda that I wanted a Crystal Award, I got one.

I had never given a speech before. Katherine and Lynda worked with me on my speech. And Coca-Cola sent Sandy Linver from Atlanta to teach me how to be a public speaker. It was very important to Coca-Cola that senior management be able public speakers. I was not.

Sandy worked with me for months. But when the day came, I was truly terrified. On the dais were all of the other award winners, including Eddie Olmos and Leslie Caron, and many of the most important people in the business: Victor Kaufman, Bob Daly, Tom Pollock, Larry Gordon, Barry Diller, Sherry Lansing, Madonna, Jodie Foster, Ron Meyer, Jim Wiatt, Michael Douglas, Jim Brooks, Dan Melnick, Lucy Fisher, and Penny Marshall, to name a few. There were 1,500 people in the audience, many who had been my friends and allies and many who hadn't.

I peeked out at the audience from backstage. And immediately began to sweat. There *were* 1,500 people. And I, the one who'd lost her voice in the sixth grade, was going to have to speak to them. My legs suddenly wouldn't move.

Then Nora Ephron came on to introduce me and as soon as she began to speak, I began to feel better. I'd picked the perfect person: talk about warming up the audience. She began:

Thank you all. It is my pleasure today to introduce Dawn Steel and her hair. I have been thinking a lot about Dawn's hair in recent weeks because there was an article in a New York magazine about Dawn. I'm sure some of you saw it. It talked almost entirely about her hair. It quoted her hairdresser, a person with apparently only a last name, who said people pay "homage" to her hair. This is a warped way of looking at things but it made me realize that we have had two women studio presidents in recent years and both of them have had major hair. What does this mean? Is it like that thing where you can have anchor women but only if they're blond? Should we be worrying about this? Is it one of those deals where we're going to have to say women will only truly be represented in the film business when we have a woman studio president who is bald like the guys? I don't know, but I did want to take an opportunity, speaking of all this, to introduce you to two very special people who are here today who will give you a clue that you don't just go out and buy hair like this, you are born with it. I want you to meet Dawn's parents, Lillian and Nat Steel. Will you please stand up?

My surprised mother and father stood up, with their two heads of thick hair. Everyone applauded them.

By the time Nora was finished, she had put the audience in the palm of my hand.

I began:

This is the second award I've gotten this year. The first, which was given to me by *California* magazine for being one of the worst bosses in the state, is shared with nine other persons, one of whom received it for trying to flush two of his employees down the toilet. I didn't deserve that award and I don't deserve this one. But getting this one makes me feel a whole lot better about getting that one.

The audience roared. They were with me all the way. The next thing I knew, I was telling them about all that had led me to this moment, telling them about how I had wanted those Pappagallos in every color.

19

AWAKENINGS

AFTER THE WRITERS' STRIKE BLESSEDLY ENDED, VICTOR, Lou, and I were able to implement our plan and make Columbia a place where talent wanted to be.

It was at this time that Amy Pascal gave me the script of *Awakenings*.

I loved this script. I could see the movie immediately. I could see the cast. The only thing I couldn't see was a way to get the script out of Fox.

The script had been developed at Fox. Penny Marshall was attached as its director. But Fox was iffy about making it. They didn't think it was commercial. But Penny had gotten Robert De Niro to agree to play the patient, but Fox, it seemed, was ambivalent about that, too.

I called Penny and Walter Parkes and Larry Lasker, the producers, and told them I was so moved by this script, and with Penny's vision of it, that we would make it with anyone they wanted (something no studio would *ever* say to any producer or director, if that studio was smart).

After months of Amy and me badgering Penny, Walter, Larry and Penny's agent, Todd Smith, after months of phone calls and never giving up, Fox finally and reluctantly let *Awakenings* go.

Every studio in town went after it. But because I had made them that offer they couldn't refuse, we got it.

In 1990, Victor combined Columbia and Tri-Star. Not only did I have one studio reporting to me, now I had two. That year we released *Look Who's Talking, When Harry Met Sally, Casualties of War, Postcards from the Edge, Flatliners* and *Awakenings,* among others.

Flatliners was the first movie Michael Douglas produced under his overall deal at Columbia. (You remember *Romancing the Michael.*) And the movie actually made his deal very successful for us. *Flatliners* was to become one of the most profitable films in Columbia's history. The profit-to-cost ratio was huge, particularly because the back-end participation was virtually nonexistent; none of the cast was yet a big movie star. (Of course, a year later, they would be.) Except for Michael Douglas's gross participation as a producer, all the other players were net participants. And as I said earlier, according to David Mamet, "There is no net." We were able to put virtually all the profits in Columbia's pockets.

Because Victor, Lou and I were in fact able to relight the torch, the combined Columbia–Tri-Star box-office share that year was 16 percent, which put us in third place, but in reality we were a small fraction from being in a three-way tie for first with Warner's and Universal.

The combined studio was now much more attractive and viable. Sony came back.

And so did the rumors—the rumors that Sony would buy Columbia–Tri-Star, and the rumors that I would soon be dead . . . again.

I kept remembering that old poem, "If—": "If you can keep your head when all about you are losing theirs and blaming it on you . . ." I couldn't.

I was exhausted. And my exhaustion with simultaneously being a mother, a wife, and an executive under fire exacerbated my mood. Which was bad. More fodder for the press.

I had a recurring nightmare. In it, every assistant and every secretary I had ever worked with and fired appeared together on *Geraldo*. The theme of the show was "I survived the boss from hell." I woke up in a sweat.

And what was worse, I was unhappy. I was becoming increasingly aware that I didn't like the job. This was a horrible realization for me. I had worked since I was fifteen years old; I wanted to be a somebody. I had become a somebody. And I didn't like who I had become or what I was doing. *My grandmother used to say, "Be careful what you wish for. You just might get it."* Her words were coming back to haunt me.

Jeffrey Katzenberg loved his job. He always loved his job, from the moment I met him. Mark Canton, who would ultimately replace me at Columbia, loves his job. He always loved his jobs. The lesson: In these jobs, you had better love what you're doing. And I didn't.

The very thought of giving up this job terrified me more than almost anything I had ever experienced, because my entire identity was wrapped up in my job title. If I wasn't *this,* who would I be?

As the rumors flew that Sony was buying us, the word on the street was that I was being fired and that Walter Yetnikoff was taking over. (He of the erection-as-measurement-of-success theory.) Yetnikoff had been Sony's ally during the takeover of CBS Records and had been Chairman Norio Ohga's friend for many years.

The rumors were making it very difficult for me to do my job. Talent was hesitant to commit to movies at Columbia because they didn't know whether they'd be working for Victor and me or for Walter Yetnikoff.

At seven A.M. Monday morning, September 25, 1989, Victor called me and said, "We've sold the company to Sony." My first question was not "How much money have I made?" It was "Are you staying?"

If he was going to stay with the company, out of loyalty and appreciation, I would have to stay, too. But if he was leaving, I could leave as well.

He answered, "I can't discuss it yet."

But I knew. In my heart I knew. As painful as it was to accept, it was time for me to move out of the corporation and back to my entrepreneurial roots. To hold my nose and jump. To know when to hold 'em, to know when to fold 'em. I knew it was time for me to leave.

Ten days later, Victor decided to leave. So did Lou Korman.

I was ready to resign.

So I waited, and I waited, and I waited to tell somebody that I wanted to go, but no one even talked to me. Not about my job, not about leaving, not about staying.

It was like the moment you decide to break up with an unfulfilling boyfriend. You've had enough. The next time you talk to him, you decide, you are telling him it's over. You have finally gotten up the guts to end this thing, once and for all, and then he doesn't call you.

So I was literally stuck holding the phone.

Meanwhile, the search was on for the sixth Columbia administration in as many years.

I was, in effect, shut down. Neither my staff nor I had any idea who would be in charge of Columbia's future. The whole company was in a holding pattern.

First Sony offered the job to Mike Ovitz, who turned it down. Yetnikoff was pushing for his old friends, Jon Peters and Peter Guber, to head the company. At the time, they were highly successful producers exclusive to Warner Brothers.

Warner Brothers didn't want to let them go. And in a much-publicized corporate battle, Peters and Guber secured their release and became co-chairmen of Columbia Pictures. But it would cost Sony a fortune in payments to Warner Brothers.

Sony, inexperienced in Hollywood etiquette (an oxymoron, at best), neglected to ask Warner Brothers Chairman Steve Ross for permission to negotiate with Jon and Peter. This little mistake cost them more than $200 million. I wasn't the only one with lessons to learn.

I was in my office in a meeting with a young woman who wanted advice about how to break into the business. Boy, was I the wrong person to ask that day. All I wanted to do was break out.

Suddenly, in mid-conversation, the door burst open and Jon Peters flew in. All of Jon's emotions were bigger than life and this day, they were bigger than usual. He picked me up, threw me over his shoulder, twirled around, marched out the door. "Come see Peter!" he said. "Do I have a choice?" I asked, from his shoulder.

We went down one elevator stop, into the conference room where Peter Guber sat surrounded by accountants. When Jon finally put me down, we all hugged and kissed, except for the accountants. The last time Peter, Jon and I worked together was on *Flashdance,* many lives ago. We went back a long way. And our feelings of affection seemed mutual.

Jon and Peter made it clear they wanted me to stay. And, for a few days, I put my desire to resign on hold. These were people I knew, people I had fun with. I wondered if the job would be any different with two very hands-on, creative filmmakers in charge. I wondered if there was any chance we could work together.

But in the first production meeting, it became clear that was not going to happen. Peter, known to be the fastest-talking person in the United States, was quiet. Jon, on the other hand, had an opinion about everything. But most of his opinions were that he hated most of my movies. Loudly and categorically, he hated them. If I hadn't been so exhausted, I would have been humiliated. But I was furious.

The specific doesn't matter. But shortly thereafter, Jon canceled one of my projects, without telling me. I called him on it and fled to New York.

I was in my New York office when Jon called, screaming. "Let me make something really clear. You work for me. You report to me. Everyone reports to me. Everyone who works for you reports to me."

And I said, "Jon, read my contract. That's not the way it works."

He said, "I don't care. Get it!" and he hung up.

The next thing I knew, Chuck got a call from my former lawyer Tom Pollock, who is head of Universal. "I just had the most bizarre conversation I have had in the history of my career in the motion picture business," Tom said.

He said Jon Peters had called him and had insisted that he—Tom—get hold of me to tell me that I had to report to Jon. Tom said Jon had screamed, "You tell her she has to report to me. You tell her she works for *me!* You tell her things have changed."

And Tom Pollock very quietly said, "Why are you telling this to me?"

"Aren't you her lawyer?" asked Jon Peters.

"No," said Tom. "I haven't been her lawyer for years. I'm chairman of Universal Pictures."

And without missing a beat Jon Peters said, "Well, what did you think of the grosses last weekend?"

I had been here before. Been here. Done that. There was only one thing for me to do. Good-bye, good luck, break a leg.

20

RESHOOTING
THE ENDING

PETER GUBER MADE IT POSSIBLE FOR ME TO SETTLE OUT MY
contract. And in January of 1991, I left Columbia.

It was ironic to me that among the last movies I
green-lighted were *Flatliners* and *Awakenings*. *Flatliners* was about med school students who wanted to
experience death. *Awakenings* was about a catatonic
patient who was desperate to experience life.

It was time for my own awakenings.

The higher I went up the ladder in corporate life,
the less creative it was, the less fun it was, the less it
was about movies and the more about budgets and
board meetings and administration. For me it was
hell.

So when Michael Eisner and Jeffrey Katzenberg
called and said, "Dawn, come home," I ran to Disney.
I did not pass Go. I just ran.

I was going to be a producer for the first time, with my own production company. And going back to Michael and Jeffrey made me feel safe. After all, they had really raised me at Paramount, I thought. It was like going home to Mom and Dad.

The first day of my new job, I drove to the Disney lot in Burbank; of course, I got lost. When I finally arrived, there was a line of cars in front of me. I was totally unaccustomed to waiting in line. At Paramount and at Columbia, I was always waved through the traffic. This was the first time in years I was stuck in it.

When I got to the gate, the guard stopped me. "Hi," he said, "who are you going to see?"

"I work here," I said.

"Oh. Who do you work for?" he asked me pleasantly.

"Me," I said, and in a very small voice, "I'm a producer."

I wanted to shoot myself. I was reminded of the morning, many months before, when I had seen Gene Shalit reviewing *Postcards from the Edge,* one of our movies at Columbia. He said, "Rob Reiner is brilliant in a cameo as a sleazy producer." He paused and added, "But that's redundant, isn't it?"

As I drove to my new parking space, I realized I was about to embark on a whole new career. Again.

Sly Stallone had phoned me right after I left Columbia. I said, "Where have you been? It's been ages."

He paused. "I've been shedding my skin," he said.

As I parked my car, I knew exactly what he meant. I was shedding mine, too.

Disney was known to be the cheapest studio in Hollywood. Their tightfistedness was legendary. Often, they paid writers and actors and directors less than any other studio in town. It's their way or no way. And they're proud of it.

I, luckily, was able to negotiate a great deal. I had beautiful offices. I had a great parking spot. I had discretionary funds, for both expenses and development. I was happening.

I hired a staff, a great staff. Assistants, development people, and Chris Meledandri to be president of my company. But I had come from Columbia with nothing, no scripts, no movies ready to go. I really was starting from scratch.

I began to look for projects. I met with writers, I had lunch with agents, I watched old movies to see if there was something I wanted to remake. Within a year, I had six or seven projects in development, two of which I thought were on the fast track to production. I was wrong.

In fact, I was wrong about a lot of things. Suddenly, from being a studio head with one hundred and fifty phone calls a day to return, I had twenty. If I didn't generate a call, I didn't get one.

I couldn't get over how hard it was to develop a script with a writer, which almost always takes twice as long as you think it will. And then, after months of meetings and notes and rewriting, I finally handed the script to the executive in charge of the project, and no one from the studio called me. I had to wait. And wait. And I was a lousy waiter.

Now, I knew that as a studio executive, you have more than one project on your plate. You have maybe twenty-five or thirty projects, all needing your attention.

But I didn't care. This transition was a bitch. I was used to all the perks that went along with my former job titles, which included immediate attention and as immediate gratification as was possible.

But I didn't have a title anymore. Or my perceived power. For the first time in my Hollywood career, there was no "Vice-President of Production" after my name. No "President of Motion Picture Division" after my name. I was simply "Dawn Steel." I was just another producer. I had gone from being a Youpeople to one of "thosepeople." I felt naked and vulnerable.

And getting a movie made was much harder than I had ever thought. As an executive, I made the decisions about what movies should be made and with whom. As a producer, these decisions were no longer mine. They were now being made by the youpeople.

For the first time in my career I understood how difficult and how painful it was for all the producers and writers and directors who had struggled to get their movies made when I was an executive.

I had to ask Jeffrey for everything. Everything. "I'd like to make the movie with this director," I'd say.

"I don't like him," Jeffrey would say. "How about so and so?"

"You won't make it with X, but you'd make it with that *hack?*" I'd say.

287

Jeffrey had this infallible logic. "I won't make you do anything that you don't want to do. And you don't make me do anything I don't want to do." Checkmate.

"I'm confused," Mike Ovitz had once said to me. "I'm confused," I'd say to Jeffrey.

And I'd leave and go back to the drawing board till our next encounter. I was feeling unproductive. And frustrated. And impotent.

I was working on a script I had loved for a long time. It was a small movie but I was determined to get it made. Even though Jeffrey turned down some of my directors. Even though one of the studio executives put it in turnaround until Jeffrey changed his mind. Even though the studio made me cut three million dollars out of its already small budget. I was still determined to get this thing made.

It took me two years, but I finally got it green-lit.

We went into preproduction, cast the movie, chose the crew, and in December of 1992, we went on location.

And there a remarkable thing happened: I loved it. I loved everything about it. I loved the sixteen-hour days, I loved the minus-twenty-five degree weather. I loved the director. I loved the cast. I loved the crew. I loved the collaboration and I loved the way I fit into it. I was happy. Who said anything about happy? I did.

For the first time in my career, I loved Sunday nights. I had no anxiety. Just excitement about what every day would bring.

I missed my family terribly. But I was suffering

more than Rebecca: she was thriving. Chuck and Rebecca had plans to come to see me every three weeks.

In fact, they were due to arrive that Friday, when I got the phone call. My mother was in the hospital. Critically ill. I had to get to Palm Beach as soon as possible.

I called Chuck and told him I was on my way to Florida. I didn't even pack. The executive producer, Susan Landau, took over for me. I left. I couldn't stop shaking.

On the plane, I kept thinking there must be some mistake. Though my relationship with my mother had certainly had its ups and downs, over the last six years, since Rebecca's birth, we had developed a really special bond. I was not prepared to let go of it.

People say that when you have your own child is when you begin to understand your mother. People are right. At least, in my case that was true. It had taken me so long to come to an understanding with my mother that I was not ready to be without her.

I arrived in Florida late on a Tuesday night. I saw her Wednesday morning. When I walked into the room, they were moving her to intensive care. She looked at me, pleadingly, and whispered, "No respirator, please."

That night in intensive care, she said to me and my father, "I know that I have been loved. And I have loved you." That was the last thing she said to us before she lapsed into a coma.

My father, my brother and I talked to her constantly during the next five days. I told her everything that I had ever wanted to tell her, about how much of a hero she was to me, about how much I loved her, how I would never have been who I was if she hadn't been my mother. I believe that she heard me. I hope she did. And there was this moment—I was holding her hand and I knew she was proud of me. It was almost as though she was sending me the thought, I'm proud of you, Dawn. I'm proud of you, too, Mom.

She died that night. I was totally unprepared for losing her. I was more devastated than I could ever have imagined.

Chuck was with me when we buried her two days later. He stayed with me in Florida, comforting me as best he could. I was almost inconsolable. Chuck had been right; cutting the umbilical cord really hurt.

The movie was still shooting. I had to go back to work.

When I got back to location I was enveloped by the crew. Rebecca came to stay with me. I needed her.

One day on the set, she met me for lunch. We were in a parking lot eating hot dogs from one of the lunch trucks. I looked at my daughter, with her mustard-covered mouth. She was having such a great time. She was already friends with the entire crew. She was laughing. And I thought to myself, "I did good."

Suddenly, I had this image of my mother. She was going off to work, dressed in one of her suits. She had to go to work. She had to take care of her family. She didn't have a job with a fancy title, or a plush office, or her own parking space. The guard didn't know her, in fact there probably wasn't even a guard where she worked. She didn't have a hundred calls a day to define her status. She wasn't looking for anyone to rescue her. She wasn't looking for power. My mother did what had to be done because the power was already in her.

And suddenly I realized that it wasn't about the powerful job with the powerful title, because if they could give you power, they could also take it away from you. I realized that in every job I had ever had, there was someone with power to give me power, someone to take care of me: Michael and Jeffrey and Diller and Simpson and Victor and Keough and Ned and Frank and Peter and Jon and Bob Guccione. I realized suddenly and finally that I didn't want to look for power anymore. That I didn't have to. Because it was already in me. It had been there all along.

And at that moment, I knew I was free.

We didn't have a year of the woman for nothing. Women are winning at the voting booth and, more and more, in the home and in the office. They are creating a new leadership style. And I don't mean by bypassing men. I mean that women have begun to forge a style that combines the best of men and women—tough and compassionate, aggressive and morally and emotionally responsible, decisive and creative.

Don't wait . . . now's the time. Make the call. Set an easy goal: Introduce yourself to one new person at a business function. Don't take rejection personally. Don't give up. Passion is the key to success. Your opinion is your currency. Speak out. Speak up. And let them call you tough.

It's not just luck. It takes work, will, repetition, risk, sometimes making a fool out of yourself, sometimes taking a huge leap of faith. But always remember— it's never too late. If I can do it, you can do it. If I can do it, anybody can do it.

Rebecca and I share a daily ritual. We call it "cuddle time." Cuddle time can occur any time, day or night. But it's our time to curl up together, to talk about the day, to watch *Nick at Night,* to listen to music, to read, or just to be quiet and hug.

Lately, I've noticed that every time we cuddle, there's another tooth missing in her smile. And what a smile it is.

Rebecca loves to read. And one night during our ritual, I read her a poem from Jeff Moss's book, *The Butterfly Jar.* The title of the poem is "WHAT HAPPENED THE NIGHT GRANDMA SAID, 'I'M SO HAPPY BEING HERE WITH YOU THAT I'M AFRAID A TRAIN IS GOING TO RUN RIGHT THROUGH THE MIDDLE OF THE HOUSE AND RUIN EVERYTHING.'"

And it goes like this:

> The train didn't come
> Grandma was wrong

> We stayed happy
> All night long

Rebecca looked up at me and smiled her toothless smile. "Isn't life great, Mommy?" she said. Yes it is, honey. Yes it is.

And every day, when I wake up, I thank God I am a woman.

AUTHOR'S NOTE

The movie I was producing that made me finally fall in love with my career was *Cool Runnings*. It got great reviews and became Disney's most successful movie of 1993. It went on to gross over $140 million at the worldwide box office. And as of May 5, 1994, it was the #1 video in America.

Acknowledgments

FOR ALL THE GIRLS I'VE LOVED BEFORE: My buds, Lynda Obst and Nora Ephron, who read and reread this book and helped me more than they know, two women whose extraordinary talent has made me look like a genius at many different points in my career, including this one. To Lucy Fisher, who knew people had been calling me mother for years, for showing me what that meant. For Nancy Collins, whose unwavering confidence in me kept me going from the beginning. For Marilyn Mordecai and Sue Ruben, who for six years made it possible for me to have a balanced life.

And for Liz Smith, who as my friend Nancy said it, believed in me before I did. And my profound appreciation, respect and gratitude to Dr. Dee Barlow, who never, ever, gave up on me. Thank you to my agent (do you believe I have an agent?) Amanda Urban, whose very gentile name belies her very *yiddisha kop*.

My reverence and awe go to my new friend, the very gifted Marcelle Clements, for organizing this life and writing a great deal of it with me. And to her very impressive support staff, Paige Williams, who made sure, come hell or high water, that Federal Express picked up the pages on weekends and holidays, and Leesa Chalk, who God knows how, figured out the proper punctuation in her very accurate transcriptions. And to my very impressive support staff, Marianne Gray and Doug Segal, who never complained once during this process. And special appreciation to Bonney Kinnick and Gabriella Schwartz, who helped me more than they know.

For Margie Glucksman Clark and Gay Bryant, who were my first two real girlfriends.

And for the girls in the "she's one of us" group, Lili Zanuck, Ruth Bloom, Gabriella Forte, Laura Landro, Lucie Salhany, Marilyn Vance, Deborah Morris, Barbara Benedek, and Lisa Specht, who taught me more about friendship among women than I could ever have learned on my own.

AND FOR ALL THE BOYS I'VE LOVED BEFORE: For Barry Diller and Michael Eisner, without whom I'd still be in the toilet paper business. Thank you to Bob Guccione, Craig Baumgarten, Don Simpson, Jeffrey Katzenberg, Victor Kaufman and Ray Stark. And for my friends Howard

Rosenman, David Geffen, Sandy Gallin, Bruce Weintraub, Larry Mark and Jim Wiatt for being as proud of me as my parents were, and maybe more so. And a big hug to my lawyer, Jake Bloom, who continues to keep me out of trouble (no small feat).

My deepest appreciation to my father and to my brother for allowing me to tell their stories honestly.

For Jon Turtletaub and Susan Landau for making my first filmmaking experience one of pure collaboration and joy. You have truly spoiled me for the future. And a special thanks to Lisa Kasteler for watching my back and for not being afraid to give me advice that I wasn't going to like.

I've been thinking for three years about how I would thank my editor, Judith Regan, whose idea this was, and who stalked me like I stalked talent in my world, who nurtured me and encouraged me in a way I had only given and never received, whose editorial judgment, input, and encouragement have made this book what it is. It is an understatement to say that this book would never have happened without Judith.

To great bud Katherine Reback, who read every draft of this manuscript between writing speeches for candidate Bill Clinton and writing scripts, gave me great notes, ideas and insights, but so much more importantly, helped me find my own voice, which had been lost for so long, and did it without judgment or criticism. Katherine Reback, your part in this book is immeasurable, and I thank you from the bottom of my heart.

And finally and most importantly, for Chuck, whom I love more each day, and who supported me and advised me through the most amazing last eight years. Its no coincidence that all the really good stuff happened to me after I met him.